T0290491

MATTHEW BARNABY

UNFILTERED

MATTHEW BARNABY
UNFILTERED

Matthew Barnaby
with Kevin Shea

TRIUMPH
BOOKS

Library of Congress Cataloging-in-Publication Data available upon request.

This book is available in quantity at special discounts for your group or organization. For further information, contact:

Triumph Books LLC
814 North Franklin Street
Chicago, Illinois 60610
(312) 337-0747
www.triumphbooks.com

Printed in U.S.A.
ISBN: 978-1-62937-987-6
Design by Nord Compo
All photos are courtesy of the author unless otherwise noted.

I'd like to dedicate this book to my family, friends, and fans who have stuck with me through the good times and the bad. May none of us ever give up on our dreams.

CONTENTS

FOREWORD

EVERYBODY WHO PLAYS IN THE NHL has a story of where they are from, how they got there, and what kept them in the league. Matthew Barnaby was one of those players with a story that should inspire any boy or girl to never give up on their dreams.

Through sheer grit and determination, Matthew defied all odds to become an NHL player. Hidden behind the combative style he displayed was a player with great hockey sense and an underrated skill set.

Matthew was not perfect and made mistakes like us all, but what I found in Matthew was a person and teammate who loved the game, competed every night, and displayed courage that inspired his own teammates to play harder for each other.

Mark Messier
Hockey Hall of Fame, Class of 2007

FOREWORD

MATTHEW BARNABY'S STRENGTH isn't limited to his win-loss record or penalty minutes. His true strength lies in his character, and that number is off the charts. I've never met someone so committed to living—really living—every single day, and his passion for life is contagious.

He's kind and considerate, and even when he doesn't have it, he makes time for everyone.

A true class act.

Eric Lindros
Hockey Hall of Fame, Class of 2016

PREFACE

THERE I WAS, sitting on the bench, my heart pounding. I could feel the sweat dripping down the back of my neck. My palms were sweaty. This was it. I could hear the crowd cheering. I had rehearsed this moment in my mind about a million times in the last few days. Then I got the tap.

I hopped over the boards. I knew I had to do something to stand out. The puck dropped, and I went right after the toughest guy on the ice. The rest is a blur, but I know I got my ass handed to me.

The crowd went nuts!

We all have a defining moment in life, and this was mine.

I was 148 pounds, a fish out of water, and wanted something so bad that I would do anything to get it.

People say they are willing to do anything, but are they really?

CHAPTER 1

"YOU'VE DONE WELL"

I WAS PLAYING IN MY 14ᵀᴴ NHL SEASON. At times, I would reflect back on what my brother told me before my first Junior camp: "If you're going to make it, you've got to do something that'll make you stand out!"

I was one of the least likely guys to play in the NHL. I had been cut by my Midget team, for fuck's sake. As hard as it is for people to understand, it was way harder for me to make Junior than it was for me to make the NHL. That isn't diminishing the level of play in the NHL at all. It's that I was an unlikely candidate to make Junior—cut by previous teams, not yet fully developed physically, still learning my role—whereas I had progressed much further by the time I was 19 and drafted by Buffalo.

A *Hockey Night in Canada* feature in 1998 called me the "most unpopular player in the NHL." I had found my role. I was an agitator. I was always chirping, and I often said things on the ice that I shouldn't have. It got me in trouble sometimes. It put a target on my back. But I loved entertaining, and people paid a lot of money to watch us play. I wanted the fans who came to watch us play to feel like they got their money's worth.

Between Junior and the NHL, I'll bet I fought 400 times. I'm six feet tall and 190 pounds, and there were times when I was the only guy who fought on the team, so every game I had to face the heavyweights: Bob Probert, Tie Domi, Donald Brashear. I took more than my share of punches to the head, but I hung in and tried to get my licks in when they were getting tired. But while I'm most remembered for chirping and fighting, I could also play. When I got ice time and didn't have to look over my shoulder all the time, I could score and put up some points.

On December 20, 2006, we were in Anaheim to play the Ducks. At 6:26 of the first period, I got into a fight with Shawn Thornton. Shawn is a tough guy. I had played with him in Chicago and tried to convince management to keep him with the big club because it would take some of the pressure to fight off me.

We started to throw some punches. I got a couple of licks in, but he pulled my helmet off and landed some punches to my head. We ended up against the end boards, and the linesmen approached us to break up the fight but just as quickly backed away. Shawn hit me a few more times and we wrestled until the officials stepped in.

I went to the locker room, put ice on my head, and took a couple of Advils. I couldn't see out of my right eye. I was near the end of my career, but I didn't want it to end that way. The trainer came into the room and asked if I was okay. I said, "Yeah, yeah. Let's go!" When I went back out for the next period, I still couldn't see out of that eye, so I asked my other winger if we could switch sides so I could play on the right side so I could see the ice better. In the third period, I got into a tussle with Shane O'Brien and ended up getting a game misconduct.

I continued to play but had headaches for the next several days. A couple of games later, on January 9, 2007, we played the Phoenix Coyotes at home in Dallas. I kept it quiet, but I had a massive headache and still couldn't see out of my right eye after the scrap a few games before. At 11:18 of the first period, Josh Gratton challenged me. We were right in front of the Coyotes bench. He could really throw them, and hit me with a couple, knocking my helmet off. I still couldn't really see out of my right eye, but I tried to hang in and got a couple of punches in. I waved off the officials and we kept going. The linesmen finally stepped in and broke us up.

I played through the rest of the game and took a couple of Advils. My wife was driving us home after the game. We were on the highway and I told her to pull over. I was puking on the side of the highway. I had a brutal headache when we got home.

I went to the rink the next day and told the team I couldn't practice. I had terrible headaches the entire week. I sat down with Dave Tippett, our coach, and Doug Armstrong, the general manager, and told them that I couldn't play. They sent me back to Buffalo to see Dr. Elad Levy, one of the top neurosurgeons in the United States.

We put together a DVD compilation of my fights before my appointment. Dr. Levy just looked at me. He was absolutely serious and said, "It's taken a toll, Matthew. Maybe you never got knocked out, but the punches you have taken throughout your career have accumulated. You can't go on like that. You've done well, you're a smart guy, and you want to see your kids grow up."

My kids were more important to me than anything in my life. I knew in my heart what Dr. Levy was saying. I was done. It was the end of my NHL career.

CHAPTER 2

NEIL HEWSTON

I NEVER KNEW MY FATHER. I never really put much thought into it. I had a loving family—my mom was a single parent, my brother is 14 years older than me and in many ways was a father figure to me, and my grandmother was a big part of my life too. We were all very, very close growing up. I had aunts and uncles as well, but it was my mother, brother, and grandmother who were my family. I never asked my mom anything about my father, and to this day, I really don't know anything about him.

I was born in Ottawa on May 4, 1973. The name on my birth certificate is Neil Barnaby, but *Neil* is crossed out. I have no idea why. Maybe Neil was someone in my father's family.

Although I never knew my father, I have learned that his name was Dwayne Hewston. I didn't even know his name until a year or two ago. Not once through my life have I asked about my father. During my NHL career, we players had to talk to psychologists, and on several occasions, they would ask me about my father and the impact his absence may have had on me. I would tell them sincerely that I never cared. He was never in my life. Going through life without a father has never made me sad, even when I was a kid. I might have thought about not having a father around Father's Day, when all the other kids in my class were making things for their dads, but other than that, I never thought about him.

I never asked his name or anything about him. People might find that strange, but that was the way it was.

To go even deeper, Barnaby isn't even my actual last name. I guess my name should actually be Neil Hewston after my father, or Neil Simmons, which is my mother's maiden name. Barnaby is actually the last name of my brother's father, but that guy was never in the picture either. Maybe my mom wanted her boys to have the same last name; I don't really know. It's a question I've never asked.

Although I didn't have a father, I had a great mother, a great brother, and a great grandmother, and they gave me a great life, so I never, ever questioned it. I'm Matthew Barnaby, and that's good enough for me no matter what the story is.

Through the years, several half-brothers and half-sisters have reached out to me. My birth father appears to have had several families, but I am not at all close to them. None of them speak very highly of my birth father. I am close to my mom's family, and that's it. I was raised by my mom, Sandra, along with my brother, Brent, and my grandmother, Ethel Simmons. And my competitive nature comes from my grandmother more than anyone.

I never think of my brother as a half-brother. Brent is my brother, full stop, and even though he is 14 years older than me, we have always been very close. I was 11 years old when Brent got married. The wedding was on a Saturday at noon. I was a really good baseball player as a kid and played travel ball. Immediately after the wedding, I left so that I could play my baseball game. I hit my first-ever home run that day, and after we won the game, I returned for the wedding reception. Sadly, the marriage didn't last. My brother's wife accused him of spending too much time with me, watching my sports, and asked, "Are you married to your brother or to me?" That's when they split.

Anyone who knew me when I was a kid would tell you that I was always really energetic, always playing sports of one kind or another, and they would remind me that I was always a runt. I didn't grow until

I was in my mid-teens, but that never stopped me from doing well in sports. I did track and played baseball, soccer, and hockey at an elite level, and was on travel teams for the last three.

My life was sports, but hockey was what I loved more than anything from an early age. My brother was a fan of the Montreal Canadiens, so I became a Habs fan too. I may have been only four or five years old, but I could recite the members of the 1977 Montreal Canadiens and their numbers flawlessly. Brent would quiz me on the players, and I would nail them: Michel Larocque, No. 1; Guy Lapointe, No. 5; Pierre Mondou, No. 6; and on and on. By the time I was nine, Mats Naslund was my favorite player by far.

I started to skate when I was five years old as a member of the Hawthorne Saints at the Walkley Arena in south Ottawa. Around that time, we moved from Ottawa to a suburb called Nepean. By the time I was eight or nine, I was really good—not a great skater, but I was scoring a ton of goals. Because I started skating at five, I was probably a year or two behind a lot of the kids on my team. The coach went to my mother and told her that I was a really, really good player but that I needed to get help with my skating. We didn't have a lot of money, but somehow Mom found the money to sign me up for power skating. The instructor was a guy named Bucky Buchanan who had played a few games with the New York Rangers in the late 1940s. Bucky worked my ass off, and my skating got so much better.

I later went to Chris Finnerty Hockey School. He was known to work with kids whose families couldn't afford the cost of advanced training. It's not a great business model, and I'm sure it caused arguments between Chris and his partner, but Chris let me join his group on the ice for free. He was really advanced in working on skills.

My brother was never much of a hockey player, but then he never had the opportunities that I did. My mom worked hard as a social worker, but she was a single parent. We didn't have much, but we never lacked for anything. At the time, though, she didn't have the money to put Brent in hockey.

Brent is a really hard worker and makes a good living working at a lumberyard, where he has worked for most of his life. On Saturday nights during the winter, the boys he worked with used to have a pickup hockey game at 11:00 or midnight. Every single Saturday from the time I was 8 until I was 15, I either practiced or had a game earlier in the day, played some street hockey, and shot pucks against the wall at least 500 times, and then Brent and I would order a pizza and two liters of pop and watch *Hockey Night in Canada*. We'd watch the game until 10:00, and then we'd record the rest of the game. We'd head over to the rink to meet the boys he worked with, and he'd warn them within an inch of their lives not to tell us the final score of the game. Of course, they always would, just to be assholes.

When I was younger, I'd watch the guys play, but when I was about 12, I started playing with them. They were all men—guys in their 20s, 30s, and even 40s. It was so much fun! But some of the guys didn't like being shown up by a teenager, so they'd come after me. I remember one time, one of the guys came at me and Brent jumped the guy and it started a full-on brawl with guys who work together. We'd get off the ice around 1:00 in the morning, go back home, watch the end of the *Hockey Night in Canada* game and finish off any pizza that was left, and then watch the later game. We'd be up until 4:00 in the morning.

I was antagonistic when I was a kid, but it was all in fun. I didn't really fight much, but I would needle other kids with verbal jabs. I was a confident kid, probably borderline cocky. There is only one man I'm afraid of, and that's Brent. He's about 5'8" and 220 pounds. As I got into my teens, I thought I was tough. One time, I kicked him in the face and broke his nose. He told me I had 10 seconds to lock myself in my bedroom before he was going to come after me, so I ran up there and locked myself in. I remember crying when I heard him coming up to the room after those 10 seconds because he would have laid a beating on me that I never would have forgotten. I prayed to God, but Brent checked the door and then walked back downstairs. It may have been the luckiest day of my life!

From the age of 10 on, there weren't many days when I wasn't on the ice at least once a day. I really loved it. But I was also playing competitive baseball and soccer, so no matter what the sport was, I was always on the best teams for my age.

When I was 11 or 12, I played on a competitive soccer team as well as a competitive summer hockey team. One time, I had a soccer game at 10:00 about an hour outside of Ottawa in the Valley, and then I had a hockey game at 2:00 in the city. I never thought much about it and suggested to my mom that we rent a plane to get me to and from these games. It should have dawned on me that it took my grandmother's help to even allow me to play hockey, never mind renting a damn plane! But I was a kid. I didn't know! I was even on the phone calling aviation companies to find out if there were planes available. It didn't get very far before my mom called them back and told them to pardon the previous call but they were talking to an overeager 12-year-old!

My school was about a mile from our house, and starting when I was 13, I'd walk to school. In the winter I'd bring my skates. There was a shed at the school, so I'd leave my skates there, and over the lunch hour, I'd go for a skate on the outdoor rink. Sometimes I'd go back to school and sometimes I wouldn't. Just like so many other kids, I'd be on the outdoor rinks from the time school ended until I got called in to eat or it got dark.

I never really liked school. Life, for me, was hockey, even at a young age, and school was secondary. I got by and did my homework, and my grades were fine, but I didn't really pay attention to school. I do have one teacher who really stands out. When I was in fifth grade at Leslie Park Public School in Nepean, there was a teacher named Mr. White. He was the gym teacher and the soccer coach. I did it all—gymnastics, cross-country, soccer. For two years running, I was the student athlete of the year at Leslie Park. Mr. White loved how competitive I was—I *had* to win no matter what I did! Feeling sorry for other kids was not in my psyche. I had no shutoff valve. (By the way, his son, Todd White, who was a couple years younger than me, went on to play in the NHL too.)

My family just didn't have the money to go on vacations. For me, a vacation was getting to play hockey. When I was 12 years old, my summer hockey team traveled across Canada for 10 days playing exhibition games. We had an incredible team; we never lost a game. From that team, 14 guys went on to play in the OHL or Division I college hockey in the U.S. and 5 guys played professional hockey.

Our trip across Canada started in Winnipeg, then we went on to Calgary and Edmonton. From there, we took a train to Banff and then went to Vancouver to play. I was a small kid but was confident and energetic and always joking around. We were having some fun in the pool on an off-day, and one of my teammates, Andrew Brodie, pushed me and made me cry, so I went up to my room. My brother was there. He looked at me and asked, "What the fuck's wrong?" I told him that Andrew had pushed me, and he was a lot bigger than me. My brother gritted his teeth and said, "Quit fuckin' crying and go back down there and punch him right in the face."

I went down to the pool, the tears still streaming down my face, and I punched Andrew as hard as I could. It drew a bit of blood. I got a lot more respect after that. The guys didn't tease me as much. It wasn't a defining moment, but it sure opened my eyes that day. It made me realize that I didn't have to put up with anybody's crap anymore.

I was still pretty small when I was 15. I was on a pretty lousy summer hockey team. We had a practice at Potvin Arena in Gloucester on the east side of Ottawa at about 10:00 at night. After the practice, I had a quick shower, and then my brother was going to drive me home in his red 1980 Chevette. By then it was around 11:15. My brother said, "You didn't work very fuckin' hard tonight. You were fuckin' the dog out there." I just looked at him and told him I was the best player on the team and could go half speed out there and still be better than anyone else. I was being cocky as hell with him.

We got into a fight in the car when we were about eight minutes along on the Queensway, the main east-west highway that goes through Ottawa. I yelled, "Fuck you!" "Oh, yeah? Fuck you!" he yelled. He told me to get the fuck out of his car. I did, and he started to drive away really slowly, and then I saw his brake lights come on and his door opened. "Hurry up. Get back in the car!" he yelled. I told him to go fuck himself, so he got back in the car and drove home. We were in front of Earl Armstrong Arena, which was also in Gloucester, and I had to get to our home in Aylmer, Quebec, about 45 kilometers, or 28 miles, away.

It was 11:30 and pitch-black. There I was, 15 years old on the side of a highway. I had no money, and we didn't have cell phones back then. I walked all the way to Carling Avenue—about 15 kilometers, or 9 miles, away—where my grandmother lived. It took me about three hours, and I got there about 2:30 in the morning. I can assure you, my mom and brother had a big fight after that.

By that fall, I was having an incredible season playing Minor Peewee. I ended up with something like 215 points. I was the best player on the team, but our coach played mental games with me. There would be times when he would be nice to me because I was helping the team win, but other times, he would berate me and tell me that I was selfish. I think he was angry because he had a kid on the team who wasn't all that good, while I was getting the points and the accolades. He repeatedly told me to pass the puck to his son. It was tricky because if I had a break, I'd have to wait for his son to catch up. If I didn't, I'd get shit from the coach, calling me selfish and saying that I only cared about myself.

We were playing in a December tournament in 1985. In the first two periods of a game, I had two goals and an assist and we were up 3–1, but I got sent to the dressing room because I celebrated after a goal. While I was taking off my equipment, our trainer came into the room and told me to hurry and get dressed because the other team had tied the score and the coach wanted me back on the ice. I scored two more, and we won the game. Even though I had four goals and an assist, the coach continued to berate me. The best player at the end of the tournament was awarded a $1,500 scholarship toward future education. Each coach had to submit the name of one player on his team who deserved consideration as their most valuable player, and then the tournament officials would select the player who would receive the scholarship. Our coach submitted his son's name even though I had 18 more points in the six-game tournament than his kid. The tournament officials called my mom and told her what had happened, and they told her that they were going to award me the scholarship despite what our coach had done.

In another tournament a month or so later, we were playing the Gloucester Rangers. I was racing for the puck for a breakaway, but my friend Steve Thornton, who was playing for Gloucester, caught me and we both went flying into the end boards. His skate cut right through my shin pad and split my kneecap. I skated back to the bench in some pain, and when the trainer asked me if I was okay, I told him that I was all right, but my knee felt like it was burning. I played the rest of the game, but I was in great pain and was hobbling around.

After the game when I was taking off my equipment, I took off my shin pad and our goalie, Jamie Pilkington, had to run because he was going to puke. My ligaments looked like they were hanging out of my kneecap. My mom drove me to the emergency room, and it took 20-some stitches to sew me up, and they put a full leg cast on me. I was out of commission for two months.

In my first practice back, we were doing a military drill called a bear crawl to work on our core and our leg muscles. In the bear crawl, you get down on all fours and walk across the ice and back keeping your knees off the ground. It was my first day back on the ice after two months off post-injury. I had a doctor's note that said I could begin skating lightly to start but that was it, so I went to the coach and told him I couldn't do the drill, but he insisted. "I don't care," he said. "You're going to fucking do it!"

I tried so hard and got about halfway down the ice, but the pain was brutal and the tears were streaming down my face. I was in agony. The coach yelled at me to keep going and in front of the team told me that I was never going to amount to anything in hockey because I was a pussy. I was 14 years old, for fuck's sake! I did the best I could, but the coach kept berating me.

My mom had dropped me off at the rink. Some of the other parents witnessed what was going on, and they called her. By the time I got off the ice, my mom was already in the dressing room with the coach and manager. She was irate! She's the nicest person in the world, but when she loses it, look out!

The coach took out his teeth and pulled up his pant leg to show my mom his scars and said, "This is what it takes to make it to the pros." My mom just looked at him and said, "If you think I want my 14-year-old to look like you, you are wrong!" We vowed that I'd never play hockey for him again.

That caused animosity, as you can imagine. I was going into Minor Bantam, and I didn't want to play on his team, so I asked for a release. I was refused. They told me I could go to A hockey instead of AA, but they refused to release me. There were very few options, and mental abuse wasn't regarded the same way as it is today, so my mom made the decision that we would move. We moved to Aylmer, Quebec, which is now part of Gatineau. It was located across the river from Ottawa and is where my mom was raised. As a result, I could change hockey associations, and I played in Aylmer for two years, until 1990.

I started high school at Philemon Wright High School in 1987. School still wasn't very important to me. I knew what I wanted to do with my life, so I didn't take it very seriously. I was in the bottom third of every class at school, and I didn't really care. Growing up in Ottawa, which is a bilingual city, I was terrible at French. All of my friends spoke English.

Even when we moved to the Quebec side, my school was all English speakers. About half of the kids on my hockey team in Aylmer were French, but the kids on my team who I hung out with spoke English. I never learned French until I moved to Quebec City to play Junior.

A lot of things motivate you. When I was in 9th and 10th grades at Philemon Wright High School, Mrs. Hoefsmit, my science teacher, used to make fun of me for saying I was going to play in the NHL, so when I made the Sabres in 1992 and was interviewed on *Hockey Night in Canada,* I made a point of thanking her for telling me I wasn't going to go anywhere in life; it was real motivation.

I still hadn't grown very much. I was about 5'2" and 120 pounds, which was pretty small compared to other 14-year-old kids. I didn't hit puberty until late. At 15, I reached a crossroads. Even though I was a talented player, I got cut from my Minor Bantam team because they thought I was too small, and the next year, I got cut from my Major Bantam team for the same reason. Those were humbling moments. I realized that I was never going to play professionally, so I debated whether I should quit the game. I felt like a loser. I got a job at the lumberyard with my brother, but after a day of working there, I realized that I sure didn't want to do *that* for a living. Working 14-hour days of hard labor in the sun was not for me. I decided to keep working at hockey and see where it took me.

I ended up playing BB, which would be the equivalent of A in Ontario. By the way, my coach was former NHL goalie Michel "Bunny" Larocque. His son Stephane was on the team with me.

I tried out for AAA Minor Midget in 1990 and got cut again. I went to play AA with a coach named Michel Charron. He was a disciplinarian, but he was the right coach for me at the right time. He really appreciated how much I loved hockey. I was the most talented player on the team, and he let me be me.

I had just turned 16, and I had a growth spurt and sprouted about a foot in a year. I invited one of the guys on my team, Kirk Schoenherr, to sleep over at our house. Kirk was a really good-looking kid a year older than me, and he was the best player on our team. While Kirk was at our house, I didn't bother to do my homework, and when my mother confronted me, I talked back to her. She told me I wasn't going to play in the game that night. I was so pissed off! I was hoping to get drafted into Junior. I had 93 points in 39 games, and teams were looking at me.

Because Kirk was staying over, we had to drive him to the game that night, and my mom was going to go in and tell the coach why I wouldn't be playing. While Kirk was getting ready to go, I was throwing stuff around and telling my mom to fuck off. She said, "I don't care what you do, you're grounded. You are not playing hockey tonight!" I couldn't believe that my mom was making me miss hockey! Tell me I can't visit friends, tell me I can't watch TV, but don't take away hockey!

While my mom was getting ready to drive to the rink, my brother told me to shut up, and he put me in an empty hockey bag, then put the bag in the trunk of our car. It was a 20-minute drive to the rink. We got there and my mom went and talked with the coach and told him I wouldn't be playing. While that was going on, Brent let me out of the trunk and I went into the arena through a back entrance.

Because they were there already, my brother suggested he and my mom stay and watch the game. While Brent and my mom were sitting in the stands, I went to the coach and told him I had gotten things straightened out with my mother and I was okay to play. We went out for the warm-up and my mom asked my brother, "Who's wearing Matthew's No. 9?" My brother just started laughing. He explained how he had snuck me into the rink and that it was me out there playing. Needless to say, even though I played the game, I was grounded immediately after.

CHAPTER 3

MR. IRRELEVANT

I HADN'T MADE MINOR OR MAJOR Bantam because of my size. At 14 or 15 years old, I was 5'2" and about 120 pounds. I was skilled but really small compared to most guys my age. I couldn't keep up. I didn't get drafted my first year of Junior eligibility. The next year, at 16, I had a growth spurt, as I mentioned, and was playing AA but didn't make the AAA team. I did get called up, but I loved the team I was playing with, the Hull Midgets, so I decided to stick with them. I had 93 points in 39 games. I was skilled, but it helped that I had a great coach who really let me be me and play my game, and that was the reason I got to Major Junior Hockey.

When I was 17 years old, I decided to go to the Quebec Major Junior Hockey League draft in Montreal on May 26, 1990, but left the draft after the 18th round. I was so upset that I didn't get drafted that I left and went home. I was resigned to thinking that my career was over. Maybe I could play some Tier II Junior or get a scholarship to a U.S. university, although I didn't love academics and my grades weren't great. It wasn't until the next day when I went to practice for summer hockey that someone told me I got drafted. What? I had ended up getting drafted last overall. Last overall. When it came to Junior hockey, I was Mr. Irrelevant. There were 20 rounds back then. I was the 198th pick—the very last guy selected. I was really surprised but really happy. Because of conversations I'd had with some of the Junior teams, I thought I was going to get selected a lot earlier.

I didn't give a shit that I had been drafted last. *I was drafted!* I went to the Beauport Harfangs, an expansion club. All the stars aligned at that point. I had never heard of Beauport and didn't know what a Harfang was, but I was determined to make the team. I did some research and found out that Beauport was a suburb of Quebec City, and a Harfang was a snow owl.

I worked really hard all summer and was ready for training camp. I was so excited to get drafted and took a Greyhound bus to Quebec City for training camp. The coach, Alain Chainey, picked me up at the bus station. He had been an assistant coach with the Quebec Nordiques for three seasons, and when the Quebec Major Junior Hockey League (QMJHL) added Beauport to the league, he was hired as the team's first coach. I didn't know it at the time, but Alain Chainey would turn out to be one of the most important people in my life.

When he picked me up, Alain looked me up and down. I didn't look like your typical hockey player. I was 5'11" and weighed 150 pounds. I'm sure that being the last pick in the draft, he must have been thinking, *This kid is never going to play*, but on the car ride to camp, I told him, "I am going to make this team. You are not going to be able to cut me." I'm sure he figured that I didn't stand a chance.

There were a lot of things going against me. I was small, inexperienced in everything—including hockey and life—and I didn't speak French. The Harfangs were an expansion team. There were 19 players picked before me, plus a bunch of veterans. My chances, candidly, were not very good. There were no games in the first couple days of practice. I was doing all right in the drills, although I couldn't turn to my right. I was a good enough player that I could deke to my left, but the right was my weak side.

On my third day of camp, I called home, and my mother and brother told me that they were going to come up to Quebec City to watch me play in the intersquad games. I told them they shouldn't come because I was likely not going to make the team. I told them that the other guys were too big and strong. My brother told me, "You have to do something that will make you stand out." That sentence really resonated with me.

I had never been in a hockey fight. It just wasn't a part of my game when I played youth hockey. I asked one of the guys on the bench, "Who's the toughest guy here?" He pointed to a guy named Guy Lefebvre. He was a 20-year-old guy who was 6'3" and probably 215 pounds. To me, he looked to be 6'7" and 320 pounds.

I was a skinny 17-year-old kid. I sat on the bench, the sweat dripping off me. I knew what I had to do. I went out on the next shift and said, "You wanna go?" He must have been licking his chops! He said, "Yeah!" So we dropped our gloves and took off our helmets, and he proceeded to beat the shit out of me. I just wanted to make the team so badly that I'd do anything. When we stepped out of the penalty box, I went up to him and said, "Do you wanna go again?" He smiled, we dropped our gloves and helmets, and he beat the shit out of me again.

Between periods, we went to our rooms, and when I came back down, on my first shift, I went right over to the other team's bench and said, "Who wants to fuckin' go next? Let's go!" I can't remember who I fought, but we went at it and I got the shit beat out of me again.

Over the course of the next three days, I fought 13 times. And I lost every single time. People thought I was crazy, but I was getting recognition. I would do absolutely anything to make that team. At the end of camp, Alain Chainey came up to me and said, "We're only going to keep 20 players, but I want to keep you as an extra player. I'll work with you as a project. I don't know if you'll dress for every game, and if you do dress, I don't know how much you're going to play, but we love your attitude and how you refuse to quit. You're a crazy motherfucker! Congratulations; you've made the team!" He called me Little Kamikaze. He had gone to the general manager and gotten permission, because keeping me on the team meant extra money for school and a billet family, or host family. The GM had given him an extra spot for me.

I was forced to learn French when I arrived in Quebec City. I arrived at 17 years old and discovered that every single person was French except me. There were three English-speaking guys trying out for the team, but Alain Chainey traded two of them away, so I was the only one left. The two other guys were better hockey players than me, but Alain didn't think they were good for my development. He saw something in me that made him gamble on adding me to the roster.

Alain spoke some English, and there was another guy who spoke a little bit of English, but I was a fish out of water. In my two and a half years in Quebec, I never heard another person speak English. When I was trying out, my billet family didn't speak a single word of English.

I was forced to learn a bit of French if I wanted to eat or if I wanted to get laid. Besides hockey, those were the two most important things to me. I'd give a girl a little, "*Comment ça va? Je m'appelle* Matthew," and I could see that they loved that I was trying. While staying with my billet family, at a meal, I'd sit down and there'd be nothing in front of me. Everybody else would be eating. They insisted I learn French. They'd hold up a potato, and I'd have to say *patate* and then they'd bring a potato to my plate. But I wouldn't have a fork to eat it, so they'd hold up a fork and I'd say *forchette*, and then they would put one in front of me. Anything I wanted, I had to ask for in French. They didn't understand English, so they would just hold up objects. That's how I got the basics of French.

Making Junior was the hardest thing I ever did, and my most exciting moment in hockey. Making the NHL was easier than making Junior. By the time I was 19 or 20, I expected to make the NHL. I had started to grow, found my confidence, put up big numbers, and had fought in every game. I didn't even think about the NHL when I was going into Junior. It's not like I was a first-round pick, with the *Hockey News* predicting where I was going to go. I was the very last pick in the

Junior draft, for fuck's sake! I was a long shot to make Junior. But I was determined. Nothing was going to stop me. That was my defining moment. That defined who Matthew Barnaby is.

My roommate was Jim Bermingham. He was drafted by the Detroit Red Wings. I saw Jim talking to a guy one day and asked who he was. Jim said, "That's my agent, but don't worry—you'll never need one."

Asshole.

Bermingham was one of the English-speaking guys who got traded away. And then, like I said, I was the only English player left on the team, even though I never spoke English for my three years there.

I came out of training camp and was so excited. I had the Tackla tracksuit and the leather Harfangs jacket, and I wore them like a rock star. I moved into my billet's home, ready for the season to start.

We played at the Arena Marcel-Bedard, in a rink called La Petite Cabane—the Little Cabin. We'd get 2,000 fans at our games. Half were smoking and all of them were drunk, and they loved fights. Man, did they love fights. And they loved the way I played. I became a cult hero from the start of the season even though I was only playing two or three shifts per game.

My first game in the league was against the St. Jean Lynx, and I didn't play a single shift. I wanted to go home. It was great that I had made the team, but what was the use if I wasn't going to play? I went into the coach's office to talk to him and tell him I wanted to quit if he wasn't going to play me. Alain Chainey said, "If you quit now, you're going to quit whenever life gets tough." He told me that he really liked me, but I had to be patient. I talked to my mom and brother, and they also convinced me to stick it out.

I met my first girlfriend at my first game with Beauport. Her name was Valerie, and her father was the mayor of Beauport at the time. He was dropping the puck for the ceremonial faceoff. During the national anthem, she was right behind our bench. I looked up and she looked back at me. She waited for me after the game, and we started dating and were together for three years. She spoke a little bit of English, so she helped me learn French. Being around her and her family helped me pick up the language. I heard it all around me and watched a lot of French TV. It took me about six months to even understand some simple vocabulary and about a year to be comfortable enough to have short conversations. I am always going to struggle with whether nouns are masculine or feminine, and my grammar will always be awful, but I learned enough French to go on television and be comfortable enough to do a one-hour show with the host and have the viewers understand what I was saying.

One of the first games I played in the league was against Laval. Remember, I was about 150 pounds. We went into their rink and were losing 6–1. I challenged their bench and got the shit kicked out of me. I went back to our bench and yelled, "It's time for you guys to wake up!" Coach Chainey realized more than ever that my attitude made me stand out from most players.

Every time I got on the ice, I ran over a goalie or did some shit to stir up the other team. I fought in every game. Sometimes I fought in the warm-up! The crowd would go crazy and would chant my name. I loved it! I'll bet I fought 50 times that season, and I don't think I won a single fight.

I quit school during my first year of Junior. I didn't have a car, so it took me about 45 minutes and two bus transfers to get to my Quebec high school. That lasted five days. It's not that I loved school anyway, but it was just too hard to get to. Instead of going to school, I would go to the rink, work out, and then go out on the ice and skate. The coaches would come out and do drills with me. This is where I learned how to turn right. They'd set pylons out, and I would work hard at turning to my right. I fell so often, but eventually I got better through practice. And I worked on my shot while I was there, and it got better too.

I went home at Christmas, and my mom asked me where my report card was. I lied through my teeth: "Oh, they send it by mail. I just don't have it yet." At the end of the school year, my mom asked me the same question and I gave her a similar answer. By the time the next school year started, she realized that I was no longer going to school. I had quit. By focusing solely on hockey, I put all my eggs into one basket.

When I was home in Ottawa that Christmas, all my buddies were home for the holidays from wherever they were playing—Division I colleges or the Ontario Hockey League—and they were all doing good things. I was a bit embarrassed because I didn't have any points—no goals, no assists. I had about 150 minutes in penalties at that point. I went back to Beauport after the holidays, and along with our top scorer, Eric Cool, and our goaltender, Marcel Cousineau, I was the most popular guy on the team. Me, a guy with zero points!

I continued to fight. I was just trying to survive. I got hurt later in the season, but I ended up playing 52 games and had 9 goals and 5 assists for 14 points as well as 262 minutes in penalties. At the end of the season, there was a little awards ceremony for our team, and the fans voted me Most Popular Player. I was pretty proud that my first season played out that way.

I was excited to get back to Ottawa to see my family and friends. I had a sense of pride that I hadn't had before. When I thought about how far I'd come, it was pretty remarkable: cut from my team at 14, cut from my team at 15, cut from my team at 16, last pick in the Junior draft, and there I was a year later winning Most Popular Player on a Major Junior team!

That summer, I worked my ass off. I was only about 150 pounds, but I wanted to add some bulk. I ate and I ate and I ate. Every day, I drank a blender-ful of ice cream with Ovaltine. Every meal, I had to sit there until I ate everything on my plate. It would be hours sometimes, but I eventually ate it all, even if it was cold. I didn't belong to a gym, but I improvised. I had some workout stuff in the basement, and I ran every single day. I'd also put my brother, who weighed around 190 pounds at the time, on my back and walk up the steep steps in our house to build up my legs. I gained about 15 pounds and was a different player when I reported to training camp for my second season. I was made an alternate captain.

In my second season with Beauport, I went from playing a few shifts each game to playing regularly on the third line. Sometimes I was bumped up to the second line, and I was getting some power-play time on the second unit. And I fought every single game again that season—at least once and sometimes twice. I had a good season. I played 63 games, scored 29 goals, and had 66 points, which was second highest on the team. And I led the league in penalty minutes with 458. I was playing a significant role on the team. I was becoming even more popular with the fans. I was fighting and scoring, and I was a leader on the team. And I was the only English guy on an all-French team in an all-French city in an all-French province.

I hadn't thought about the upcoming NHL Draft for one single second, but at Christmas in 1991, I started getting phone calls from my brother saying, "You're in the paper! You're on the NHL Central Scouting list!" Central Scouting came out with a list, and I was ranked as a C prospect. I couldn't believe it! We were talking the NHL now!

My coach talked to me and explained that NHL teams were interested. They were coming to see me play. I got really excited. There were two of us attracting attention—me and Ian McIntyre, one of my teammates. We played a similar game, but Ian was bigger and tougher than me, and he had the same number of points as me even though he was a year younger. We were both waiting for the draft, hoping we'd get selected.

The NHL Entry Draft was held in Montreal on June 20, 1992. Brent and my mom drove in from Ottawa, and we sat together in the stands at the Montreal Forum. I didn't have an agent, but I had some notoriety, and leading up to the draft, I started to expect I'd get drafted in the third or fourth round. I had meetings with a few teams. Coach

Chainey had done some scouting for the Quebec Nordiques, so I thought I might be picked by them.

Larry Carriere had scouted me for the Buffalo Sabres. He told me, "You're going to be going against men now—the Stu Grimsons, the Bob Proberts. It takes a different animal to do that." In my last meeting with Buffalo, John Muckler, the head coach, asked me, "What's going to happen at 8:05 on a Saturday night when Bob Probert asks you to fight?" I just looked at him calmly said, "At 8:03, I would have already asked *him* to fight." That's when Larry Carriere turned to John Muckler and said, "I told you this kid was different." John then said, "If you're there where we have you ranked, you'll be a Buffalo Sabre."

In the fourth round, the Quebec Nordiques were making their selection. They stepped up to the microphone and said, "With the 76th pick, the Quebec Nordiques select, from the Beauport Harfangs—" I jumped up, hugged my mom, and was shaking hands and started walking toward the stage when I heard them say, "Ian McIntyre." Oh my God! I was so embarrassed. I quickly sat down. Ian deserved to be drafted before me, but I just wasn't thinking, and when they said "Beauport Harfangs," in my excitement, I assumed it was me. Fuck!

Seven picks later, the Buffalo Sabres picked me at 83. I really wasn't ready for it because I was so embarrassed about what had just happened. But it all worked out.

CHAPTER 4

GOING TO THE SHOW

IN JUNE 1992 THE NHL ENTRY DRAFT had been in Montreal. I was there a few days before the draft with friends as well as my mom and my brother. A lot of my friends from Ottawa were also attending the draft with hopes of getting drafted. Their families and girlfriends were there too.

Once my name got called, my mom, Brent, and I went to a party being held by the Buffalo Sabres. We stayed for a little while, and then everyone went out on their own. My mom, brother, and I went out for dinner, but then I met up with my friends from Ottawa and we hit the bars in Montreal. The drinking age was 18, and I had just turned 19, so I was ready to party. The bars were jam-packed, but we found a bar on Montreal's famous Crescent Street. I was sitting there with my friends, who were all wearing the jerseys and hats from the teams that drafted them, but I was not wearing any Sabres gear. The Buffalo scouts—Larry Carriere, Don Luce, and Terry Martin—saw me at the bar and came over to welcome me to the Sabres family. I asked them if I could buy them a beer, but they passed, saying they just wanted to say hi. They asked me why I wasn't wearing a jersey or hat like all the other young guys who had been drafted. I told them, "If you think I need a jersey and a hat to get laid in Montreal, you're very wrong. I guess these other guys need it!" They laughed, shook my hand, and went off and had a beer on their own.

After the draft and that evening's celebration, I went back to Ottawa and started training. Knowing that the stakes were high, I started taking my workouts to the next level at the Ottawa Athletic Club (OAC), where all the NHL guys from the area worked out, and I skated with Jeff Brown, Jeff Chychrun, and a bunch of the Ottawa Senators. I was determined to get bigger and stronger, which I was able to do.

It was about five weeks before Buffalo held their rookie camp for all the draftees of my year and a few of the prospects from previous years. We reported to the camp, which was held in Niagara Falls, Ontario, across the river from Buffalo. A buddy and I drove there together and went through the camp. They had us work a lot on skills, with an emphasis on power skating, before we got into scrimmage games. I knew what made me successful in Junior, so I took that exact same approach at the camp. If there were any doubters who didn't think I could perform at the NHL level, I wanted to dispel those thoughts right away. It was really exciting, but there was no doubt that I was going back to Junior. I was still only 18.

In our first scrimmage, I was on one team and Brad May was on the other. Brad had already played a year in the NHL. He was a first-rounder in 1990, so was a bit sour to have to be the only veteran at the rookie camp. I didn't know Brad May from a hole in the wall. As it turned out, Buffalo's head coach, John Muckler, had told Brad not to fight me. He knew that I would probably go after Brad, and as a veteran, Brad didn't have anything to prove by fighting. And Muckler also didn't want Brad to hurt me, a 165-pound prospect trying to impress the brass.

The arena had a standing area overlooking the ice surface. All the coaches and scouts hovered there to watch the prospects in practices and scrimmages. On the first shift, I was on the ice with Brad. The puck dropped, and I tracked him down, hit him, and squared off. "Ya wanna go?" I asked.

He pushed me away and said, "Get the fuck outta here!"

I had been warned that this was a tough dude, so I couldn't understand why he didn't want to fight me. I played a few more shifts and was hitting everything in sight, and then I found myself on the ice at the same time as Brad again. I charged at him, hit him, and squared off, ready to drop my gloves. "Let's fuckin' go!"

Again he pushed me away and said, "Get the fuck away from me!"

The next time we were out against each other was near the end of the first period. I took a run at Brad from the other side of the rink, and as soon as I got near him, he brought up his elbow and caught me right in the face. It knocked me to the ice, but I jumped up and said, "Let's fuckin' go!"

The first two times I challenged him, I hadn't noticed that Brad looked up at John Muckler, and Muckler had shaken his head no. That's why Brad had pushed me away. This time, after I got hit with the elbow, Brad looked up and Muckler gave him the nod. We went at it. Brad hit me way more than I hit him. He definitely won the fight. When we were sitting in the penalty box, he gave me a nod of respect.

Buffalo fans will remember the Fog Game on May 20, 1975, when the Sabres were playing the Philadelphia Flyers in Game 3 of their playoff series. The temperature inside Buffalo Memorial Auditorium (the Aud) was close to 90 degrees, and it combined with the ice to cause fog to shroud the ice surface. The *New York Times* reported that due to the lack of visibility, the game had to be stopped 12 times in the last half alone. Our rookie camp was exactly the same, although without the significance. The fog hovering over the ice surface was thick as pea soup, and all the prospects skated around trying to make the fog disappear. Brad May skated up beside me. I wondered what he was going to say or do, but he said, "Kid, I fuckin' love you!" I felt so good! And then he said, "I see you skating around hitting all these other guys. Just stay away from me!" A friendship was born at that moment. Brad turned out to be one of the nicest guys I have ever met.

37

When rookie camp was finished, I returned to Ottawa to work out and skate in order to be ready for the main Sabres camp. Because I had had success in Junior playing my style, I had every intention of doing the same at the main camp. That was my template for success.

I drove down to Buffalo and checked in to the Holiday Inn, where the team had us staying. All the rookies were together playing some cards and getting to know each other. On the ice, we would do our drills and it was all was very friendly, but once the scrimmages started, I no longer had any friends. It was each man out for himself. We were competing for the same jobs.

The day before training camp started, we had our medicals, and that night, there was a team dinner at the Crag Burn Golf Club. It was built on the site of the summer estate once owned by Frank Goodyear Jr. and his wife, Dorothy Knox, the daughter of Seymour Knox. Seymour Knox was the grandfather of Seymour Knox III and Northrup Knox, the original owners of the Buffalo Sabres.

We had a great dinner, and then, one by one, each of us had to stand up, say our name, and tell the group where we played the previous season. It was a way for management and the veterans to put a face to a name. I stood up and grinned, exposing my half-tooth, broken the year before. "Matthew Barnaby. Beauport Harfangs." As I was sitting down, Rob Ray yelled, "Fucking Killer!"—referring to my nickname. "He's going to get killed tomorrow!"

All the rookies looked at me with that look of, "You're in shit, Barnaby." I was nervous, but even though I had been prepared to fight Ray anyway, now there was absolutely no choice. I knew what to expect in the first inter-squad game between the team I was on and the one Rob Ray was playing for. I tracked him down on the ice and gave him a good push, and he was more than happy to oblige me. He was so much bigger than me, but we went at it and Rob gave it to me pretty good.

Because it was a scrimmage, we didn't even go to the penalty box. We just went back to our respective benches. The next time we were out against each other again, I went at him again, but he just sort of brushed me off, saying, "Fuck off!" I kept tracking him and gave him a slash on the back of the leg, and he turned around and we both dropped the gloves. He gave it to me pretty good again. I went back to my bench. I'm sure that all the guys on my team were thinking, *What the fuck is going on? This guy is getting the shit beat out of him and he keeps going back!*

Later that period, I crosschecked Rob into the boards and we fought again, but this time, while I can't say I won, I would call it even. It was a pretty good bout right along the boards. We were separated, and as I reached down to pick up my helmet, Rob sucker punched me in the face. I tried to get back at him, but they kept us apart. Welcome to the first day of training camp with the Buffalo Sabres!

As expected, when the camp ended, I was sent back to Junior, but I had a taste of the NHL, and I loved it. When I got back to Beauport, the season had already started. We had a fantastic team in my third year (1992–93)—a good goalie, great forwards, tough team. We had all the pieces. I had a great start to the season. I think I had eight points in the first three games. I was having a great time on and off the ice. But 11 games into the season, the team fired Alain Chainey and brought in Joe Hardy, a guy who had played a bit in the NHL and WHA.

Alain had been incredibly loyal to me. I wouldn't be where I am today without Alain Chainey. I wouldn't have played in the NHL and I wouldn't even have made the Beauport Harfangs if it weren't for Alain Chainey. I love the guy.

I was a third-year player with Beauport—their best player and the most popular guy on the team. We lost that night, and even though I had only been back with the team for a week, I walked into the general manager's office and said, "We've got to do something. We're a better team than this. I'm pissed off that Alain Chainey was fired. We've got to make a move." Twelve hours later, I was traded to Verdun College Francais, another QMJHL team.

I went out with my Harfangs teammate Dominic Maltais, who was my best friend, and we drank all night long, alternating between laughing and crying. "What the fuck did I just do?" I loved it there. In 19 games that season, I had scored 12 goals and had 35 points! I had 144 penalty minutes. I also had a girlfriend I'd have to leave behind. I couldn't believe it!

I packed up my stuff and took a bus to Verdun. When I arrived, I went over to the arena and walked into the locker room, not knowing what to expect. There was my No. 14 hanging in my stall! A rookie had been wearing the number, and they gave him No. 41 so I could have the number I wore in Beauport.

I met with the general manager when I arrived in Verdun. He said, "We're so excited to have you!" He asked me how much I had been paid in Beauport, but before I could answer, he said, "I don't care. You were traded for a 20-year-old player, so we'll pay you what we've been paying him." I looked down at the figure—$250 a week. They also gave me bonus money: $5 for every point and $5 for a plus. I said, "That will do just fine." I had been making $46 a week in Beauport!

I loved playing for the Verdun College Francais under Alain Rajotte. The team lived in college dorm rooms, usually two or three players to a room, but I was given my own room. They gave me a bunch of coupons for food, so I ate at Mike's Subs all the time, ordering subs or pizza, and I often brought some of the other players with me and treated them with my gift certificates.

We would play on a Sunday and I'd get the shit kicked out of me by Sandy McCarthy or other guys like that, so Alain Rajotte would give me the day off on the following Monday. He told me I could pick another player and we could ignore curfew, so I usually picked Dominic Rheaume.

Midway through that 1992–93 season, I fought Steve Searles, who played with St. Jean, and got knocked out cold with one punch. I didn't know that he was a boxer. I woke up in the dressing room, and the coach asked me if I was okay to go for the third period. I said, "Yeah," but when I stood up, I fell over. "You're done," he said, and they sent me to the hospital.

I knew that I had to fight Searles again. There was pride involved. I had gotten knocked out in my home rink, so I had to do it, but I was nervous. On the three-hour bus ride to St. Jean, I thought about fighting Searles every second of the trip. When the game started, I grabbed him, and I've never beaten up anybody with so much rage.

Verdun wasn't a great team. They had been the league champions the year before, but we didn't know if we would even make the playoffs in 1992–93. I was one of the team's leading scorers, and I only played 33 games with them. I had 26 goals, 61 points, and 217 minutes in penalties. I was given a choice: I could stay and continue to play with them or, in order to help with their rebuild, they could trade me to get prospects and picks. One of the options was the Victoriaville Tigers, and I liked that idea a lot. They had a good team, but more important to me, I would be reunited with Alain Chainey, who had landed there after being let go by Beauport.

I went to Victoriaville. The talk was that we had a great shot at winning the Memorial Cup. Our best player was Alexandre Daigle, who went on to be the first overall pick at the NHL Entry Draft that summer. We finished second in our division and third overall in the league, but the Drummondville Voltigeurs eliminated us by beating us in the quarterfinal.

I was really upset and was crying. I never got much of a chance to enjoy playoff success in Junior. I was in tears in the dressing room when the coach came over and told me that Larry Carriere, the scout with the Buffalo Sabres, wanted to see me. I changed and came out of the room, wiping the tears from my eyes. My mom and brother were there to greet me, and so was Larry Carriere. "Great year!" he said. "The Sabres are really happy with your development, and while I know you are upset now and had hoped to win a Memorial Cup to cap off your

Junior career, I have some good news to give you. We're calling you up to the Buffalo Sabres. You're leaving tomorrow for Buffalo!" That was the end of my Junior career but the start of my journey in the National Hockey League.

In my last season of Junior, I scored 44 goals and 111 points and made the All-Star team, but I also had 456 penalty minutes and 45 fights! It's the one line of statistics from my hockey career that I bring up most often. It's almost impossible to be on the ice that much to get that many points. I felt good about that.

The Quebec Major Junior Hockey League was a scary league back then. In my first year of Junior, we didn't have warm-up skates with the opposing team because there were too many bench brawls. I think before they shut them down, I may have been in five bench brawls before the game had even started. The Arena Marcel-Bedard in Beauport was the first arena to have a canopy covering visiting players when they went on or came off the ice. Fans looking down from their seats at the opposing teams would douse them with beer as they were leaving the ice. Now every NHL arena covers the players' entrance and exit to the ice for that reason. Our rink was insane. The whole league was crazy!

The league was filled with tough guys. In my first season, I broke my wrist in a game against Longueuil after Donald Brashear checked me from behind. We'd go into Laval, and they had Sandy McCarthy and Gino Odjick and played in a rink nicknamed the House of Pain. They were a scary, tough team. Laval packed their rink every night because they had a great team but also because there were a lot of fights. They'd intimidate you in every way possible. During warm-up in 1991–92, Bob Hartley and Michel Therrien, the Laval coaches, stood on their bench watching, so I fired pucks at them on the bench. I started that game, and Laval started their five toughest guys. As soon as the puck dropped, two or three of them jumped me. I got cut and was bleeding, and they got 14 minutes of penalties. We had a really talented kid on our team from France, Stephane Tartari, and our coach said, "We've got a power play. Stephane, get out there."

Stephane said, "No, I'm not going out there, Coach." After the game, he went into Alain Chainey's office and said, "I don't think this league is for me. I think I am going to go back to France." Alain replied, "You know, that's not a bad idea."

I did whatever it took to give our team a chance. I fought a few goalies and got escorted out of a couple of rinks at the end of games. I got suspended a couple of times, but that was it. In my second year, I separated and dislocated my shoulder about three-quarters of the way through the year. That was my draft year, so I played through it. At the end of the season but before the draft, I was operated on in Quebec City.

Everybody asks me where I learned to fight, and I tell them I learned on the job. I got beat up over and over and over, and you start to learn. I'd practice with guys to try to learn how to get an edge. We didn't have video to watch fights, so I learned the really hard way—by getting beaten up.

CHAPTER 5

SHUFFLING OFF TO BUFFALO

I WAS STUNNED. I thought I might get called up to play with Rochester, the Sabres' American Hockey League team, but getting the opportunity to go right to the NHL was beyond my expectations. But there was one problem, and it was a big one: I went to Buffalo without a contract.

I was practicing with the Sabres the next day, but I couldn't play a game because I had yet to sign a contract. It took a couple of days, but a contract was delivered. I talked with my family and to Larry Kelly, my agent, but it was a pretty easy decision: "Give me the pen and I'll sign anything you give me."

My head was spinning. Besides my salary, there were all kinds of bonuses. For example, if I made the All-Star team, I'd get $25,000. I knew that there wasn't a hope in hell, but when you added up the potential earnings, it was something like $700,000. The reality was that in my first season, I made $250,000.

My signing bonus was $90,000, paid in three installments. Our family didn't grow up with much money. I was staying at the Hilton hotel in Buffalo. It was right near the rink because I didn't have a car. There was a Marine Midland Bank on the ground level of the hotel, and I remember showing my mom my first check. She was so pleased. She said, "Three thousand dollars! That's wonderful!" I said, "Mom, look closer. There's an extra zero there." Neither one of us had seen $30,000 like that before.

I bought a car right away, a green 1993 four-wheel drive Toyota 4Runner SUV that I absolutely loved. I was so proud of it. About a month later, I put a down payment on a house in Kanata for my mom and my brother, who was living with her. She had been renting up to that point.

April 13, 1993. Surreal. In my mind, I had played out what it would be like to play in the NHL, and the reality was nothing like what I had imagined. It was a million times better! I'd visualized the scenario a million times, but there I was playing on the same ice as Pat LaFontaine and Alex Mogilny with Grant Fuhr in net and 15,000 people in the stands—including my mother—watching us play against the Montreal Canadiens, the team I grew up idolizing. Chills went down my spine. Pinch me!

During warm-up, it didn't feel real. It felt like I was in a movie. Once the puck dropped, I could only wonder, *Am I supposed to be here?* But then I found the right headspace and accepted that I was indeed supposed to be there, and I readied myself to play the way that had gotten me to the NHL. Although I had 111 points in Junior that season, I had to adapt my role somewhat. I was there to hit guys, finish my checks, and—if the situation warranted—drop my gloves for my teammates. I got into my first NHL fight in the first period against Sean Hill, a six-foot, 200-pound veteran who had played in the Olympics. I just wanted to get the first fight out of the way. Even though we ended up losing 3–2, that first game was beyond anything I could have dreamed of. In fact, it was way, way more.

In my second game, we played the Philadelphia Flyers. In the second period, I scored my first NHL goal on a power play from Dale Hawerchuk and Randy Smehlik, beating Tommy Soderstrom. Later in the period, I took Ryan McGill into the boards hard. While we lined up for the faceoff, he slashed me, and we ended up fighting. He head-butted me, and besides a slashing minor and a fighting major, he got thrown out of the game for "intent to injure." It was the final regular-season game for Buffalo that season, and we ended up losing 7–4.

We were the underdogs in the opening round of the playoffs. Buffalo finished fourth in the Adams Division, and we had to play the Boston Bruins, who had finished first in the division and second overall in the league that season. We surprised everybody, eliminating the Bruins in four straight games, three of which went to overtime. No Sabres fan will ever forget Game 4 with Rick Jeanneret's "May Day!" call when Brad scored to end the series and move us forward to face Montreal.

I had yet to play in the playoffs that spring. It was thrilling to be there whether I was in the lineup or not. I was surprised and pleased when I was told I'd dress for Game 4 of the series against the Canadiens on May 8. We were down three games to none. I earned my first playoff point with an assist on a first-period goal by Ken Sutton and picked up a couple of minors, including a roughing penalty with Lyle Odelein. I didn't play much after the second period. I was sitting on the bench, raring to get the tap, and Rob Ray said to me, "Kid, you're not playing another fucking shift." Yuri Khmylev scored with 10 seconds to go in the third to tie the game at 3–3 and take us to overtime. I went into the training room, and there was Rob Ray eating pizza and chicken wings. He invited me to join him. When overtime was set to start, I went out to the bench with barbecue sauce on my jersey. Montreal scored in overtime to win the game and sweep the series.

* * *

When you get called up and are added to the roster at the end of a season, you're looked at as an extra guy, but when you make the team out of training camp and are on the opening-night roster, you're part of the team.

We had an awesome team in Buffalo in 1993–94, led by Pat LaFontaine, who was the epitome of a captain. He treated everyone—and I mean everyone—as though they were stars. If you needed advice, you could go to him. He realized we were nervous coming into the league, and he put us at ease. But he was simply an outstanding player and just very sincere and nice.

John Muckler was our coach when I started. As tough as he was, he was really fair, and he liked me a lot. And I was surrounded by amazing guys. I got to be tight friends with Brad May, who is such a great guy. Brad had a girlfriend and spent a lot of time with her, but Rob Ray was single, so I hung out with him a lot. Those two were the guys from the team who I hung out with most. The Sabres were an older team: Doug Bodger, Keith Carney, Dave Hannan, Dale Hawerchuk, Charlie Huddy, Craig Simpson—all great guys. After games, the older guys went home to their wives and families and the younger guys went straight to the bar—a different one every night. We had a circuit: Razor's, the Stuffed Mushroom, Jim Kelly's Network, and Toons. We had a lot of great nights at those places. The Sabres played the game as hard on the ice as we partied off the ice. We went at it pretty damn hard.

We used to go to the Stuffed Mushroom on Monday nights because we seldom played on Tuesdays. I remember going there after I first got called up. I walked up to Iceman, the doorman, who was about 6'6" and had a big handlebar mustache. He just looked at me and said, "Killer! You're not 21!" I said, "No sir, I'm not." He said, "That's okay. You're a Buffalo Sabre. Get the hell in here." I walked in. The bar was open until 4:00 in the morning, and I was there until they closed.

The first night I went out in Buffalo that season, a group of us went to the Locker Room, including Rob Ray, who had just had knee surgery. I wanted to buy a round of beers for the guys, but I couldn't find Rob. When I stepped outside into the back alley, I saw a bunch of guys wanting to fight Razor. On an ordinary night, he was more than capable of taking care of himself, but he was on crutches, for fuck's sake. When I stepped in, five guys charged at me—I don't think they had any idea who I was—and I reeled around and punched one of them as hard as I could. The other guys kicked the shit out of me. My brand-new watch was gone, my new Hugo Boss suit was ripped, and I was bruised everywhere. I didn't know who these guys were, but a few years later, I found out that they were friends of my future wife, who I hadn't met yet. They were the toughest guys in Buffalo, and you didn't want to mess with them.

We were on the road to start the 1993–94 season. Our first game was in Boston on October 7. I scored in the first period that night. It was the Sabres' first goal of the season, and we went on to beat the Bruins 5–3.

Our home opener was on October 10 against the Hartford Whalers. There I was, in the runway at the Aud, and when I heard my name over the PA and skated out of the tunnel, I had goose bumps. All I could think was, *Don't fall!*

John Muckler was a stern, really tough, old-school type of guy. He was no-nonsense but very fair. Although he really liked me, he was also really hard on me. He catered to the stars—Mogilny, LaFontaine, Hawerchuk.

At one of my first practices with the Sabres, I tried to dangle Doug Bodger, one of the veteran defensemen on the team. Muck blew the whistle and called everyone to center ice. As I skated in, all I could think was, *Fuck! What did I do?*

Muck looked right at me. "Barney! How many points did you score in Junior last year?" I told him, "I scored 111." I was pretty proud. He then asked how many goals I scored. "I got 44." He said, "That's great. Now dump the fucking puck in next time. You're never going to get that in the NHL."

The veterans were chuckling, and I figured I was going to be sent down to the minors. Next shift, I dumped the puck in and ran over Doug Bodger. He just looked at me like, "What the fuck are you doing?" I shrugged, "The other way wasn't working."

* * *

I played with the Sabres through October, but then I got sent down to Rochester. I used to call Brad May "Silver Spoon" because he was a first-round draft pick and never played a day in the minors. I, on the other hand, was the Human Yo-Yo. I made the trip up and down I-90 between Rochester and Buffalo in 1993–94 and 1994–95 more often than the Kardashians change NBA players.

There were a lot of ups and down—quite literally—between Rochester and Buffalo. The Rochester Americans of the American Hockey League were Buffalo's top farm team. Whenever I was sent down to Rochester, I felt like I was disappointing my family and letting them down. But when I look back on my career today, Rochester was incredibly important to my career. The jump from Junior to the NHL is huge. You go from playing with and against boys to playing with and against the best players in the world.

I spent part of two seasons in Rochester with the Americans. The AHL is a great league, but back then it was very tough. The real difference between the AHL and NHL is you have a little more time to make your plays in the AHL. But the minors are a grind—three games in three nights, riding the bus, making $30,000 a year and fighting guys who are just as tough as the guys in the NHL. The only difference is that they can't skate well enough to make the jump to "the Show." But tough? Holy fuck, there were some crazy nights! Cape Breton had Link Gaetz, the Missing Link, who had 140 penalty minutes in 21 games in 1993–94. Cornwall had Serge Roberge, who had 342 penalty minutes in 1994–95. The list goes on and on.

In Buffalo I played limited minutes, but in Rochester I was a top-six forward earning power-play time, yet I never strayed from what I was going to be in the NHL: an agitator who'd fight when needed. My goal was to prove every night that I belonged in the NHL and not in the American Hockey League.

Rochester was a great place to play. Our motto was, "Play hard, party hard." The Americans had great fans, a great building, awesome jerseys, and a fantastic bunch of guys. When I went up to the Sabres, I was a really young guy in a room of veterans, but in Rochester most of the guys were prospects and about the same age. The veterans on the team were there to help us win but also to show us what it was like to be a professional hockey player. I played with so many great guys. Jody Gage and Scott Metcalfe were two seasoned veterans, both legends in Rochester. My roommate was Doug MacDonald, who had come to the Americans from the University of Wisconsin. Philippe Boucher had been a first-round draft pick for the Sabres in 1991, and Jason Dawe was a second-rounder that year. We were all competing to get called up to Buffalo, but we were all great friends.

Although my time in Rochester was great, I was always thinking about Buffalo. My memories of Rochester are a little blurry because we would always go from practice to Hooters or the Buffalo Distilling Company for beers and tell our buddy Billy Benz to let the cute waitresses leave work early so we could take them out. His response was always, "Sure, but make sure they're back here for their shift in the morning."

We played Friday and Saturday nights and Sunday afternoon every week, so Sunday was "green light." That meant that everyone ended up at a great pub called Preps, where we partied like rock stars on a college budget.

Guys aren't as worried about suspensions in the AHL as they are in the NHL. For one thing, the fines are a lot less but also, there are fewer cameras to catch offenses. I remember clipping Brian Curran with a high stick when he was playing for the Cape Breton Oilers. It was purely accidental. He was bleeding everywhere. I got kicked out of the game and Curran ended up getting stitched up in our training room. I was getting undressed when I heard him say, "I'm going to kill that fucker, that pussy piece of shit!" Our dressing room was 20 feet away, so I walked over and said, "I'm right here, fuck head! Let's go!" He went to get off the table with the doctor standing there, needle in hand and thread hanging from his eye, and I jumped him. We wrestled and ended up throwing punches in the hallway with our skates on the cement. Security guards were trying to break us up, and they finally did, but it was just like another day. Today it would be a year suspension. I don't remember either of us getting anything. Crazy how the times were!

In February 1995 a bunch of my teammates in Rochester said, "Let's go into Buffalo to watch the Sabres play!" I passed, saying, "Nah, I don't really want to go, guys." I was tired, and we had been out the night before.

I was sleeping when Scott Metcalfe and a couple other guys showed up at my apartment complex in a limo. I resisted. "I'm not going, guys. I'm tired. I don't really need to go watch a hockey game in Buffalo!" I had already played a few games with the Sabres. They persisted and I caved. I pulled on some clothes and we drove to the game, having a few beers on the way there.

We got to the Aud, and we ended up at the game on Sombrero Night, and wouldn't you know it, we were sitting in Sombrero Row. We all wore sombreros, and when "La Cucaracha" came on, the lights of the arena flashed on us dancing like maniacs. It was 1995—there was no Jumbotron, so we weren't on the giant screen. It was just some young guys having a blast at a hockey game. By the third period, we were drunk and just having the greatest time.

After the game, we went to the Locker Room, a popular sports bar in Buffalo, and we partied until 4:00 in the morning. We left, knowing that we had to get back to Rochester for a practice at 10:00. We were in the limo, so we didn't have to worry about drinking and driving, and we pulled into Rochester after 5:30 and then dropped each of the guys off.

When I got home, I saw the message light on my answering machine flashing and checked the message. It was from John Muckler, the general manager of the Sabres. The recording told me I had been called up to the Sabres and there was a practice at 10:00.

It was 5:30, I couldn't sleep, and I still had to pack my stuff and drive to Buffalo in time for a practice at 10:00. I tried to get an hour's sleep, but I was restless. I got a ride and left at 7:30 to get to Buffalo by 9:00, but I was still hammered!

I got to the practice on time, and Brad May turned to me and said, "I think I saw you at the game last night!" I said, "Yeah." He laughed and replied, "Nice sombrero!"

I said, "Maysie, I'm really struggling here. I'm still drunk." He said, "Don't worry. I've got you," and he took some of my shifts just to cover for me so I wouldn't look like an idiot.

*　*　*

I ended up playing 35 games with Buffalo that season, and while I didn't get a lot of ice time in games, I still was able to contribute in a way that helped the team by getting 106 penalty minutes. Pat LaFontaine missed much of the season to injury, but guys such as Dale Hawerchuk and Alex Mogilny had strong seasons while Dominik Hasek and Grant Fuhr combined to allow the fewest goals in the NHL that season. We finished fourth in our division and faced the New Jersey Devils in the first round of the playoffs.

In Game 4 I fought Mike Peluso in the first period. He got five minutes, plus we both got unsportsmanlike penalties. In the third, Rob Ray and I fought Ken Daneyko and Peluso. We all got tagged with majors, and Daneyko and I got game misconducts. We won that game 5–3. In the next game, things settled down, but we lost 5–3.

Game 6 was a classic. It was scoreless going into a fourth overtime when Dave Hannan scored on Martin Brodeur at 5:43 to give us a 1–0 win. Hasek stopped 70 shots; he was unbelievable in that game.

I didn't play in the deciding seventh game, and we lost 2–1 to end our season.

The NHL Awards that year saw Dominik Hasek win the Vezina Trophy as the NHL's best goalie. Dom and Grant paired to win the Jennings Trophy for allowing the fewest goals against, and Dom also won the Hart Trophy as the league's most valuable player. Although Dom wasn't a favorite in the dressing room, there was no doubt that he was an amazing goalie.

*   *   *

I went home to Ottawa after that and trained all summer, but I also partied harder than I should have. My agent was handling my finances, and he called me after seeing my credit card bills. "I hope On Tap is the name of a gym, Matthew. There are a lot of charges from a place called On Tap." On Tap was a bar that we went to very often, and we went hard there that summer.

Before I went back to Buffalo for training camp, I had a fight with my brother. He told me I hadn't worked hard enough in the off-season and was probably going to get cut. As it turned out, there was a lockout in 1994–95 and I got sent down to Rochester and played half a season with the Americans in the AHL. After the lockout was resolved, I got called up to play with the Sabres again. Playing with Rochester was actually a blessing in disguise because it kept me in game shape and I was there with a bunch of the young guys learning the pro game.

I never played for Rochester again. It was the start of my time as full-time member of the Buffalo Sabres. From February 12, 1995, I never played another game in the minors.

That season, I moved in with Rob Ray. We had started out at odds with each other but soon became great friends, although we had a love-hate relationship. We are complete opposites: I love fashion, while Razor wears the free T-shirts people give him. He's a hunter and fisherman, and I get my meat and fish at the grocery store.

I remember one time Razor wanted to watch the Discovery Channel, but I wanted to watch MTV. He was holding the remote, so I grabbed it from him and he went berserk. He threw me through the screen window and knocked my teeth out! We would regularly beat on each other and then go out and drink some beers. Living with Rob was like living with your brother. We'd try to kill each other, but we always liked each other.

We hung out with a bunch of the young guys—Jason Dawe, Scott Pearson, Mike Peca, Ken Sutton. We all lived in townhouses within the same development. We called it Melrose Place because the party would always end up there.

We lost a couple of key guys to injuries. Pat LaFontaine and Dale Hawerchuk both missed half the season, but Donald Audette, Alex Mogilny, and Wayne Presley helped us offensively, and Hasek was really strong in goal. Rob Ray had 173 minutes in penalties to lead the team. I was second with 117, but I played half as many games as Rob did.

Buffalo finished fourth in the Northeast Division, and we started the playoffs against Philadelphia. I didn't play against the Flyers that spring, and they eliminated us in five games.

I worked out really hard during the summer but also had some fun. There was no bigger star in Buffalo than Jim Kelly, the quarterback of the Buffalo Bills. Kelly is one of only three players to have his number retired by the team, and he has been inducted into the Pro Football Hall of Fame. Every summer, Jim held a golf tournament at the East Aurora Country Club to raise funds for his Kelly for Kids Foundation. On June 11, 1995, I was invited to be one of the celebrities. There were a ton of football players there as well as my teammates Jason Dawe, Brad May, Craig Muni, Rob Ray, and me.

Because I could be a little rambunctious on the ice, some people found it impossible to believe that I never did drugs. I never did. Not once. I would go out with the boys a lot, but it was for good times with some beers. Usually lots of beers. Did I mention girls and beers?

After the golf tournament, most of us went to a hole-in-the-wall bar called the Big Tree. The Bills hung out there after games because it was right beside Rich Stadium, where they played. It's a crazy, crazy spot.

We were all partying, drinking, and doing shots. I was headbutting Tony Siragusa and Jerry Ostroski, close friends of mine from the Bills. Those guys are massive, but it was just a great time. Around 2:00 in the morning, a guy whose name I won't mention said, "Barney! I've got a present for you in my truck!" I thought, *Fucking right! I'll bet I'm getting a signed football!* I was really excited! He told me that he left it for me in his truck, and to just go get it. The truck was unlocked.

I went out to his truck, and on his middle console there were three lines of cocaine and a rolled-up dollar bill. I was like, "Holy fuck!" I like to party, but I immediately turned around and went back in. I found Rob and Brad and told them what had just happened to me. We were immediately sober and said, "Let's get the fuck out of here!" We snuck out so no one could see us, and we went to Taco Bell.

That was my only run-in with drugs of any kind through my whole career. I was known as a wild man on the ice, but you'd be surprised to know that I never saw drugs through my entire time in the NHL, and this time, it was at a football event, not even at a hockey event. I've known people who were users, but it never interested me, and it just wasn't around. We partied hard with the Sabres—really hard—but drugs weren't part of our fun. In fact, fun was our drug.

CHAPTER 6

THE NOLAN YEARS

THERE WERE A LOT OF CHANGES going into the 1995–96 season. It was our last season at the Aud, which had been Buffalo's home rink since they came into the league. In 1996–97 we'd be playing in a new rink.

John Muckler, who had been coach and GM in 1994–95, decided to surrender the coaching portfolio. He hired Ted Nolan, a guy who had played in the Show but who had really developed as a coach after his playing career was done. He took the Soo Greyhounds to the Memorial Cup three seasons in a row and won it all in 1993. He was an assistant coach with the Hartford Whalers in 1994–95.

Ted remembered getting the Whalers job offer: "My brother asked me, 'What are you going to tell those NHL guys that they don't already know?' That was probably the first time in my whole career that I got a little intimidated. I started wondering, *What* am *I going to tell these guys?* They had the best of training, the best of coaching, the best of everything their entire careers, and there I was, a rookie coach, coming in trying to inspire them. But once I got to camp and met the guys, they were just like me—normal guys looking for direction and encouragement.

"I am not sure whether John Muckler hired me or whether Doug Moss, the president, hired me. I met with John, but I got the feeling that he wasn't really crazy about me coming in as coach, but Doug Moss and I talked the same language. We had a great conversation. Everybody talks about how hockey is a contact sport, and I remember mentioning to him that ballroom dancing is a contact sport and hockey is a collision sport. He liked that! And I told him that we wanted to entertain the fans. If they were paying all that money, I certainly didn't want them to leave disappointed. That was the attitude we took with our team, and we got known as the hardest-working team in professional sports. We had character on that team, personality on that team, but more importantly, we had good human beings on that team."

Ted came in and really believed in me. He reminded me of my Junior coach, Alain Chainey. You couldn't ask for a better coach for the style that I played. He really solidified my role as an NHLer. We had tough teams in a city that loved the way we played. We played hard, we partied hard, and we had a great bond between players.

"We worked hard," Ted remembered. "We competed like a son of a gun. We were only at the rink an hour or two a day, but our practices were intense. I was a blue-collar type of guy that believed in work ethic. It translated into games. We'd win one, and all of a sudden, the confidence was building and the attitude started developing. We weren't just playing to play anymore; we were playing to win. I told myself that there was only one thing to do in the National Hockey League, and that was win the Stanley Cup. That's what we aimed for."

I found an immediate bond with Teddy Nolan. He really understood my game. He told me, "If you look at championship teams, people have a tendency to look at the star players, which is the easiest thing to do, but championships are won with blue-collar guys. It's been that way through history and will continue that way. It's the character guys you have on your team. Coming from where I came from and having the coaching I had growing up, I wanted to be a coach for those players specifically. Stars are going to get their points and accolades, but no one is going to say 'Thank you, Matthew' because you had a great shift. You may not have scored, but you played a great shift, so I wanted to make you and guys like you as important as the superstar players. That's what I tried to infuse into the team and particularly with you.

"I remember one game, I think it was in Montreal, and you weren't having the best of games. I benched you for the first part of the third period. I didn't play you for five or six shifts. The team started coming back, and we were leading Montreal by one goal. I went to you, and I put you back on the ice to help protect the lead and get the win. Fortunately we won the game, and you came into the dressing room and talked to me. It brings tears to me even now. You said, 'Thank you, Coach. Thanks for coming back with me. No one has ever done that to me before.' Everybody has a bad game, but when you bench somebody, it embarrasses them. It was important to see how you responded to it. But that's who I am as a coach. All players need a bit of love and understanding and somebody to push the right buttons. I found your true character, as a person even more than as a hockey player."

I was supposed to have my rookie party at the Turtle in Anaheim the year before. I was on the trip, but on the bus after the game, John Muckler came over to me and told me I was getting sent down to Rochester, so I didn't get to partake in the rookie party that season. When Muck told me I was going to Rochester, I told him that all my stuff was in Buffalo and asked if I could fly to Buffalo, get my things, and then bring them to Rochester. He said, "No! You're going to Rochester." He was as old school as they come. So in my mind, I was flying to Rochester, driving to Buffalo, and then driving back to Rochester. Not logical, but John told me what I had to do. But when I got to the airport, I thought, *Fuck it. I'm changing my flight and going to Buffalo*. I think it cost me a hundred bucks to change the ticket, and I was fine with that. It saved me a lot of hassle.

When I was in Junior, a lot of hazing took place that was just wrong. I was made to drink so much that it made me puke. I was locked in the bathroom at the back of the bus with six other guys, all naked, and the veterans poured water on us and threw our clothes in, all tangled up together. We couldn't come out of that bus bathroom until we were fully dressed. Another time, we had to run naked through town. The worst, by far, was making the rookies jerk off on a piece of bread. The last guy to cum had to eat it. I'd had enough. I said no way were we doing that. The next day at practice, I warned the other rookies that something was going to happen on the ice. When the veterans came out, we jumped them. The coach asked me what had happened, and I told him, "Everything's taken care of." A few of the veterans were traded from our team.

I never saw any of that in the NHL. There was the usual rookie dinner where the rookies split the bill for an expensive team dinner. I didn't have to do that in 1994–95 because the guys wait until they know you're going to be with the team full-time, so I didn't have my rookie party until January 10, 1996, in Winnipeg. Mike Peca and I had to buy dinner for the team. Most of the team had gotten so hammered in Montreal that Pecs and I were the only ones drinking, but we ran the bill up pretty good ourselves.

But the guys pulled a prank on us. The coaches were in on it. Peca and I had slept with two girls in Buffalo. It was entirely consensual, but the cops came to the rink the next day and handed us a slip of paper. We were being accused of rape! We were leaving for Calgary the next day, so we were shitting our pants. Finally the guys told us that it was a joke. Some joke! But at least I could breathe again.

There are two things I get asked about more than anything. One is the hat trick I scored against Montreal on Mother's Day 1998 and the other is the Garth Snow fight that took place on March 29, 1996.

Garth Snow and I already had history that preceded the fight. I was playing with Rochester while the NHL players were locked out in 1994–95. We were playing the Cornwall Aces, and Garth Snow was their goalie. Cornwall had a tough team, and Garth and I got into it a couple of times and threw some punches in tight quarters near the end of games.

You always know your surroundings when you're on the ice, especially when you're playing tough teams and playing the role that I did. On March 29, 1996 against Philadelphia, I went to the net and tussled with Snow a bit as I was trying to get in front for a rebound or to screen. Shawn Antoski crosschecked me right in the ribs, and I went down. I was hurt a little bit, but I was also trying to draw a penalty. I was lying on the ground and didn't really know what was going on when, out of nowhere, Brad May went flying in like Jimmy "Superfly" Snuka of wresting fame! Our team really had a wolf pack mentality in looking out for each other. Brad clotheslined Antoski while I was lying there. Bob Boughner and Alexei Zhitnik were out there trying to get at him too, and I could hear the crowd going nuts, and I knew that there was a five-on-five brawl going on. Shit was getting real. While I was lying there, Jim Pizzutelli, our trainer, came out to check on me. Jim loved fighting more than anyone in the world. He used to go to the other team's rooms before games and set up fights with the opposing trainer. We used to call him Don King. He leaned over me and asked if I was okay. I said, "It stings, but I'm fine, Jim." He told me to stay down because there were fights all around, but I told him, "I know Garth Snow is going to come over and chirp me, so I may jump up if he does."

I was getting to my knees when Snow came over and gave me a couple of taps with his stick. I knew that everyone else was paired off behind the net, so I knew I had 10 to 15 seconds alone with the goalie, whom I hated. I jumped up and started throwing haymakers at Snow. It was in Buffalo, and I knew the fans were going to absolutely love it. Then Rod Brind'Amour came in to pull me off of Snow, and from there, it just kept going. I fought Rod for quite a while—I might have broken his nose in that fight—and our goalie, Andrei Trefilov, came charging in, and he and Snow continued that fight.

We ended up finishing fifth in the Northeast Division and didn't make the playoffs. It was the first time since I was with the Sabres that we had missed the postseason. Although I was disappointed, I was pleased with my overall season. I scored 15 goals and had 31 points and led the league in penalty minutes with 335. Brad May had 295 to finish fourth, and Rob Ray finished fifth with 287.

* * *

I had a really good year in 1995–96 and established myself as an NHLer. Ted Nolan had given me opportunities to play. I showed everybody, including myself, that I wasn't just an agitator and a fighter. I could score at the NHL level too.

My contract was up for renewal. I talked with my agent, and we had a number in mind. We wanted to sign for around $700,000 a year. John Muckler, an old-school GM, offered me three years for something like $525,000, $550,000, and $575,000. That wasn't where we were in the negotiation. When we couldn't finalize the contract, I held out. I wanted to play, and I had been on my rookie contract making $250,000. Muck called my agent and said, "Here's our final offer: $525,000, $550,000, and $600,000," and my agent told him we weren't taking that.

As much as you love your team, when you're holding out, you hope the team loses, because that gives you some leverage. The Sabres lost the first game of the 1996–97 season, and John called me directly, which wasn't something that usually happened in contract negotiations. He offered me $25,000 more and told me he had given his final offer and that if I didn't report to the team, he was going to let me rot. Intimidation tactics. "Muck, I'm not trying to be an asshole," I told him. "The number we're looking for is fair, and I want to play." We hung up, and that night Buffalo lost again. In the first five games of the season, Buffalo got outscored 18–6. We got a deal done at that point, and I was happy.

A lot had changed over the summer. The Sabres had moved out of Memorial Auditorium and we now made our home at the newly constructed Marine Midland Arena. We had new uniforms too. The old blue-and-gold jerseys were replaced with a black-and-red design with a white buffalo-head crest.

I played my first game of that season on October 24, 1996, against Montreal and scored in my first game of the 1996–97 season. We won 6–3 that night. I had a good feeling about the season, but maybe that good feeling was a bit premature.

Patty LaFontaine was our leader, both on and off the ice—a fabulous guy. He was our top scorer and our captain. In a game against Pittsburgh on October 17, Francois Leroux had hammered him with a hit to the head that knocked him out with a concussion. Patty only played 13 games with us that season, and they were the last ones he'd play with Buffalo. He was out for the season and then was traded to the Rangers for prospects before the 1997–98 season, which would be his last. Such a great, talented guy was forced to retire with post-concussion syndrome.

Ted Nolan didn't let us get down. "We might not be the most talented team, but once in a while you have to fly on your own," he told us. "There is no more Patty to get us a big goal. We have to find a way to get us a big goal on our own."

We won the next four games and were playing with confidence. "[Our guys] think they can win every night," Muckler told the press. "They have no fear of who they're playing against."

Doug Moss, the team president who gave me my bonus, was fired in November, and Larry Quinn was named to replace him. They had been disagreeing for months about how the team was operated. And John Muckler, our general manager, had been bickering with Ted Nolan, our coach, over the direction of the team. As players, all we could do was put our heads down and play the games, ignoring the stuff off the ice.

Speaking of non-game drama, we were supposed to play the Boston Bruins at our arena on November 16, 1996, but just after we had our morning skate, the Jumbotron crashed onto the ice! It was a miracle no one was hurt. The fucking thing weighed 20 tons! And it had cost

$4 million to put in our brand-new arena! We couldn't play that night, so the game against Boston was postponed.

Even if management wasn't tight, the guys on the team were, and I had guys who I liked to hang out with. One was Brad May. While having some beers with Brad the night before we played Chicago on January 20, 1997, we had a bet on who was going to fight Bob Probert, the undisputed heavyweight of the NHL, the next night. Whoever fought Probert first got $500 from the other guy. During the game, Brad went after him, so I jumped in the middle so he couldn't get the first fight and win the bet. On the next shift, I went at Probie, but Brad jumped in the middle. As we sat in the penalty box, sobering up from the night before, we realized how ridiculous the bet was. Two stubborn assholes! We looked at each other and asked, "Do we really need the $500?" As it turned out, neither one of us fought Probert.

On March 30, 1997, we were played in Chicago, staying overnight before continuing our road trip. Some of the guys were friendly with Chris Chelios, the captain of the Blackhawks. Brad May asked Chelios where we should go for a night out. Chelios said, "I've got to get my family home and get them something to eat, but I'll meet you at my place, Cheli's, and we can figure things out from there."

So a group of us—Rob Ray, Brad May, Jay McKee, and I—went over to Cheli's Chili Bar and had a few beers and something to eat while we waited for Chelios. While we were there, he messaged us about meeting him at another bar. He told us that Michael Jordan's handler, George Koehler, would take care of us there. Sure enough, George was expecting us, told us to come in, sit down, and that Chris would meet us shortly. It was a strip bar, and the girls were up on the stage dancing. All of a sudden, Dennis Rodman of the Chicago Bulls came over, and George introduced us to him. He was wearing a Chelios Blackhawks jersey. We thought, *This is fucking cool!* It was the heyday of the Bulls.

One of the girls, Mimi, was particularly hot. Rob Ray went up to the stage and tucked a five-dollar bill in her bikini bottoms. She leaned down and they kissed. When Rob came back to the table, Dennis Rodman was laughing. "Yo! Do you realize that Mimi has a bigger cock than you do?" We laughed so hard. Rob had kissed what he thought was a beautiful girl...but she wasn't!

We left there and went to a famous place called the Crobar. It was a Sunday, but it was so jam-packed and hot, and the ceiling dripped condensation. I looked over at one point and two of my teammates were in cages hoisted above the stage, and they were dancing!

I was at the bar with Chelios and Rodman and a bunch of others. Something was wrong. Within an hour, I was a puddle. I had never been so drunk in my life! I had to leave and get back to the Drake Hotel right then or I was in trouble. I had never felt like that in my life. Five of us climbed into a taxi. I was laying across three of the guys in the back seat and I started puking all over the legs of the guys I was laying on. While I was puking, I shit my pants!

I had to get the cab driver to pull over so I could puke some more. We were at a place called Cabrini Green, one of the most dangerous housing projects in Chicago at the time. Where we stopped, you could see people gathered around barrels with fires in them to keep warm. The cabdriver told the guys in the taxi, "You gotta get him back in the cab or I'm gonna leave him here! We're gonna get shot if we stay here!"

They piled me back in the taxi and we drove to the Drake, a historic and legendary hotel built in 1920 that has housed presidents and celebrities. When the cab pulled up in front of the Drake, I pulled my pants off. They were full of shit, and I had shit dripping down my leg! There is a big red carpet that leads up to the entrance, and the guys helped me get to the front desk.

I asked at reception, "Can I get my key, please?"

The lady at the desk asked me for ID. I looked down, saw my penis, and realized that I didn't have any pants on. "Ma'am, I have no pants, let alone ID!" I said. The other guys got me to my room and I fell asleep immediately.

The next day, we had a practice at 10:00 in the morning before we flew out. I was barely conscious, and during a drill, I stepped on a puck that was lying on the ice and fell. Everybody looked over and wondered what the hell was going on. Ted Nolan came over and asked, "What'd you do last night, Barney? You look awful! You're a mess!"

I said, "Teddy, I don't even know. I was so wasted. I think I got drugged!"

He said, "Okay, go to the room, put ice packs on your knees, and I'll cover for you and tell everybody you got hurt in the game."

"Thank you!"

Later that day, we boarded the plane for our next game, and from the time I got on, I threw up nonstop in the tiny bathroom at the back of the plane.

By April 1, 1997, we were closing in on our first division title in eons. People were calling us the biggest surprise of the season, and certainly the way the season began, no one could have predicted we'd be in the rarefied air of the elite teams in the league. We played the Rangers that night, and in the second period, I hit Pat Flatley and injured my left knee. I was diagnosed with a sprained left medial collateral ligament that would put me out for at least four weeks. That same night, Dominik Hasek returned to play after missing six games with a broken rib.

We finished first in the Northeast even though Patty LaFontaine, our captain and best player, was injured for most of the season, as I mentioned. Dominik Hasek was unbelievable. And even though I missed the start of the season because I held out, and then got hurt at the end of the season, I had a really good season. In fact, it turned out to be the best season of my NHL career. I had 19 goals, 43 points, and 289 penalty minutes.

We played Ottawa in the opening round of the playoffs. We took the first game 3–1, but Ottawa came back with the same score in the second game. But then things got weird with Hasek. During the warm-up before Game 3 in Ottawa, Hasek let in a few goals, got pissed off, and smashed his stick on the crossbar. He started the game, and then Ottawa scored their first goal late in the second period. Hasek went to the bench and then down the tunnel to the dressing room. We had no idea what was going on. He didn't seem to be hurt. Our backup, Steve Shields, went in to replace Hasek, and then Dom came back to the bench, but he was dressed in his street clothes. There was no sign of injury—no limping or ice packs or crutches. We won the game but wondered what the fuck was going on with Hasek. He told reporters, "I won't be back until the end of the series."

What the fuck! And then after the game, when we left for the hotel, he didn't come with us. Instead he left with Frantisek Musil, one of Ottawa's defensemen and a guy who Dom knew back in the Czech Republic. He didn't even tell Teddy where he was! We were so pissed.

Jim Kelley, a great guy and the sportswriter for the *Buffalo News*, had seen Hasek running out of the rink. He wrote, "I don't for a moment believe that Dominik Hasek intentionally bailed out on his coach and his teammates Monday night [Game 3], but I do believe the pressure of having to be unbeatable may well be more than even he can bear."

I think most of the guys thought it was a fair statement. Not Dom. He confronted Jim and called him a liar and "the worst person in the world." And then Dom grabbed Jim and ripped his shirt. It took a few people, including Jason Dawe, to get Hasek away from Kelley.

The Sabres issued a statement, calling the incident a "very serious matter," and the NHL investigated. Teddy Nolan said, "Sportswriters are going to write things that make people upset, but in society, you can't go around hitting people for these reasons. I can't condone that."

It turned out that Hasek had a mildly sprained medial collateral ligament in his right knee. The NHL suspended him for three games, but even after getting medical clearance because of what our doctors described as "residual pain," Hasek didn't play again in the playoffs. He bailed on us. I know it. I had confirmation from Jim Kelley after the series. The worst thing was holding a press conference with the entire team standing behind Hasek. We all knew that Dom had quit on us, and yet we were forced to attend the fucking conference. Most of us just rolled our eyes at the ludicrous situation.

Steve Shields played amazingly for us, and we won the series against Ottawa four games to three, but we were eliminated by Philadelphia in the next series.

There was so much turbulence on the team. John Muckler and Teddy Nolan weren't getting along. Teddy said, "There is no secret about my relationship with John Muckler. He wanted me to do some things I didn't agree with. He wanted me to play Pat LaFontaine when he was hurt, and I refused to do it. He asked me to sit out certain players, and I refused to do that too, although if somebody wasn't playing very well, I certainly would, but to sit someone out in order to play a higher draft choice didn't go over well with me. I always believed in playing the best players who were able and capable at the time. Our disagreements were well documented. I didn't back down then, and I still wouldn't do it today. I believe in treating the players with the respect they deserve."

It makes it difficult when your GM and coach aren't on the same page. We called it a *schmozzle*. The dressing room was a disaster. There was so much shit going on behind the scenes. The room was divided. Some of the guys were on Muckler's side and some chose to be Ted's guys.

We were shocked when Larry Quinn, the team president, fired John Muckler in May, one day after he was named NHL Executive of the Year by the *Sporting News*, and replaced him with Darcy Regier, who was promised that he could decide who he wanted to coach.

The NHL Awards were held in June 1997, and the Sabres swept just about every category in which we had a nominee. Dominik Hasek won the Vezina as top goaltender as well as the Hart and the Pearson as the NHL's most valuable player, and he was selected for the First All-Star team. Michael Peca won the Selke Trophy as top defensive forward. Ted Nolan won the Jack Adams Award as coach of the year.

Patty LaFontaine and Seymour Knox won the Lester Patrick Trophy for their outstanding contributions to hockey in the United States. It was a night of celebration for our team, but in the background, there were cracks in the veneer.

Around that same time, Hasek told a reporter, "It would be better for me next season if Nolan were not there." Ted Nolan was stunned. He told me, "Dominik was a total surprise to me. I didn't see it coming until I read something in the paper. I didn't know that there was a major problem. He wanted me gone. I am only speculating, but he had a good relationship with John Muckler, and that may have had a lot to do with his feelings toward me. Dom was a loyal guy to John, and he may have thought I was disrespecting John in a way, and that may have affected his thoughts toward me."

Ted was under contract until the end of June. Everybody expected that there was no doubt that he'd be back. He had just been named Coach of the Year, for fuck's sake. Other than Hasek, all the players loved Teddy.

I asked Ted to tell me what happened. "Jim Kelley worked for the *Buffalo News*. He was one of the most respected writers in hockey. He called me the night before the contract was offered to me and said, 'Ted, I understand they are going to offer you a one-year contract at the same money you had last year.' He asked me if I was going to sign it.

"I hadn't seen the contract, so I called Darcy and said, 'Our treaties have been broken in the past. My First Nation people have had misunderstandings for generations. Before, our people couldn't read. I can read. I'd like to see the contract before you say you're going to offer me one.'

"I saw the contract and I thought it was an embarrassment. I turned it down. I told him I wasn't going to sign it. He flew into Sault Ste. Marie, where I lived in the off-season, to tell me man to man that they were going to pull the contract offer off the table. I told him he could have saved himself a plane ticket and just dropped a quarter into a pay phone to tell me that.

"Bob Swados, one of the executives at the time, was on record saying that their goal was to make me an offer that they knew I would refuse, which was what I did.

"When I reflect back on those two seasons in Buffalo, they were two of my fondest. Although I didn't have a great relationship with hockey in general—with management—I had a great relationship with the players. That's what a coach is hired for: not to win games for you but to win games for *them*. They're the ones on the ice."

When I heard the news, I couldn't believe it! They brought in Lindy Ruff to replace Ted Nolan as coach. I didn't think that was right. I believed there was a conspiracy against Teddy to get rid of him. Ted Nolan was a guy who I loved—not only as a hockey coach and for what he did for me, our team, and the city but also as a person. Ted Nolan is a great human being, and once he didn't come back, I was pissed off. I was quoted in *Sports Illustrated* at the time saying that I was going to run Dominik Hasek during training camp because he had essentially gotten rid of the coach who I loved. Dom wasn't a great guy. He was a great goaltender—the best in the world at the time—but he quit on our team by faking a knee injury in the playoffs.

During the summer, Doug Moss, the team president, called me into his office to talk. He knew that I had threatened Dominik Hasek. I had a clause in my contract that said I'd get $50,000 if I hit 50 points during that 1996–97 season. Because I was injured at the end of the season, I finished with 43 points. Doug said, "I know you didn't get your bonus. You were just seven points shy, and if you hadn't been hurt, you likely would have achieved it. Here's my proposal: If you don't jump Dom at training camp like you said you were going to, I'll give you your $50,000 bonus."

Great deal! "I'm not a great businessman if I turn that down," I said. When I told the guys I hung out with on the team, they were blown away.

Doug Moss cut me a check for $50,000 and I didn't jump Dom during training camp, but after tryouts were over, I slashed him and went after him. That was the beginning of the end of my time in Buffalo.

In June 2014 the Hockey Hall of Fame announced that Dominik Hasek was to be inducted the following November. Hasek's agent contacted me and invited me to the special ceremony to witness Dom's induction. I responded, "You know I fucking hate him, don't you?" Needless to say, I had other plans for that night.

CHAPTER 7

RUFF IN BUFFALO

IT WAS A TUMULTUOUS YEAR ON THE ICE, but I had found a sense of calm and happiness off the ice. When I moved to Buffalo, I loved to party. It was vibrant and made me feel alive. I never dated very much. In fact, I had only had one really serious girlfriend, and that was in Junior when I dated the mayor's daughter. I was with her for three years. In Buffalo after games, I'd go for beers with the guys until 4:00 in the morning. One of those times, I met a very pretty, wholesome girl named Christine Cardarella. The more time I spent with her, the more I realized there was something very special about her.

Christine came from a wonderful traditional Italian family. I, on the other hand, didn't have what you'd call a traditional family upbringing, and I really loved being part of a loving family when I spent time with Christine and her family. I knew that if things ever progressed in that area, Christine would be a great mother.

Christine and I got married on June 28, 1997. We were so happy. I wasn't thinking about the turmoil with the Sabres when we went to Hawaii for our honeymoon.

Newly married, it was back to training for the 1997–98 season. But I did a lot of thinking over the summer. I loved everything about Buffalo. I loved the guys on the team. And I was a fan favorite and loved playing in front of those fans; I probably could have played my whole career there. Buffalo was all I ever knew. I went there as a young kid, drafted at 18, full of piss and vinegar, chipped front tooth and all. But I was taught at an early age that if you don't believe in something, you have to change, and I didn't agree with what happened to Ted Nolan, so I asked to be traded.

They offered Ted Nolan a one-year contract after a hugely successful season in which he was named Coach of the Year, and when he declined, they hired Lindy Ruff to take Ted's place. I didn't think that was right. I believed there was a conspiracy against Teddy to get rid of him. He is a great human being, and once he didn't come back, I was pissed off.

It wasn't Lindy Ruff's fault, but I took it out on him. In retrospect, I never really gave Lindy a chance. At the time, he already had a strike against him in my eyes. I'm a loyal guy. In Junior, when Alain Chainey was let go, I asked to be traded, and there I was doing the same thing in Buffalo.

I asked Ted to reflect on that time. He said, "Any time you go into a new situation, the coach has to prove himself to the players just as much as the players have to prove themselves to the coach. It was important that the guys knew I had their best interests at heart, and I wanted them to compete—not just sometimes but every shift.

"When I reflect back on those two seasons in Buffalo, they were two of my fondest. Although I didn't have a great relationship with hockey in general—with management—I had a great relationship with the players. That's what a coach is hired for—not to win games for you but to win games for them. They're the ones on the ice. We worked so hard, and the players took direction so well. They had such passion for the game and stood up for one another. If you hit one of them, someone was going to hit you back. I was extremely proud of that team, not only for their work ethic, but they made me proud of the organization. Our arena was packed. It was loud and boisterous. It was great to see.

"You were a young athlete giving your heart and soul to the team, the organization, and the community. You were incredibly popular. I knew you and I had a good relationship, which I tried to have with all the players, but for whatever reason, our relationship was particularly strong. Maybe it was because we both came from pretty tough backgrounds and how we both worked so hard to get to the National Hockey League, the best league in the world. And there we were competing with the best players in the world. Our loyalty sometimes gets the better of us, and trying to do the right thing hurts us sometimes. You really came out in my support. I really wanted to get a message to you: 'Hey, Matt, worry about yourself. I'll be okay.' But I don't think my words would have meant anything to you because you were so loyal.

"Sometimes with fans there are players on the opposing teams that you don't like, but I tell you, you get them on your team, and you're going to love them. You were one of those guys. Maybe the opposition didn't like you very much and the opposing coaches didn't like you, but I'll tell you, you get a guy like you on the team, you're going to love him, which I did. Unfortunately, your passion and your heart got the better of you. Those things happen, but you did go on and have a good career."

Lindy Ruff and I clashed from the start. I can now self-reflect and acknowledge that hockey is a business and that Lindy Ruff was arrogant and brought a lot of it on himself, but I can also admit that I never gave Lindy a chance. We butted heads in the locker room. He asked me a number of times not to ask to be traded, to stay with our team because he liked what I did on the ice, but I could never get over what the Sabres had done to Teddy, and I forced my way into a trade. Lindy and I had many arguments. I was benched many times, and there were many times when I told Lindy to fuck himself.

When camp opened, the players held a team meeting to address the resentment most of us had toward Dominik Hasek. We agreed to hash out the problem, but it's hard to forgive a guy who gave up on his team with a faked injury. The team had given me that $50,000 bonus with the promise that I wouldn't jump Hasek during training camp as I had told the media I was going to. I didn't jump him, but I did slash him. Great goalie, terrible guy. I blamed him for the Ted Nolan bullshit too.

We had a really rough start to the 1997–98 season. By November 20, 1997, we had only won 4 games in regulation and 2 in overtime, and we had lost 10 and tied 4. I love the Buffalo fans, but they let you know when they are unhappy, and after Hasek had had such a great season the year before, winning just about every award the NHL had, the fans expected more from him, and they started to boo him. As the season went along, the boos got louder. *Sports Illustrated* wrote, "He can't stop a beach ball, can't stop the rain, can't stop in the name of love and, most tellingly, can't stop the boos." It got so bad that the Sabres had to add cheering crowd sound effects to drown out the boos when Dom was introduced.

There was a big divide, and a lot of fans went through some tough times with Dom in that era. That was a long time ago, and when Sabres fans think back on Dom now, I think they realize that he gave Buffalo the chance to compete for several years with a very average team. I'm sure that they look back and marvel at all the great saves and things he did for the city of Buffalo.

Earlier in that season, we were playing Phoenix on October 26, 1997, and Jocelyn Lemieux hit me from behind near center ice. It's probably the hardest I've ever been hit. I didn't see it coming, and I landed face-first on the ice. I lost all my teeth again, broke my nose, and was bleeding pretty badly. Lindy ordered me to get to the locker room, but I said, "No fucking way! I'm going back out! I'm going to kill this fucking guy!" I didn't even know who had hit me. I asked our trainer, and he told me it was Lemieux.

I told Lindy to put me out the next time Lemieux was on the ice. I jumped over the boards and went right at him. "Let's fuckin' go!" He just looked at me and said, "You're fucking crazy!" I was spitting blood, my face was cut, there was blood everywhere, and my teeth were dangling out of my mouth. "Let's go! I'm gonna fucking kill you!" I screamed.

He said, "Go get your fuckin' teeth fixed. You're fucking crazy!" I continued to chirp at him, but he wouldn't fight me.

I played the rest of the game and got my teeth looked at the next day when we were in Colorado. Lindy just shook his head and said, "I don't know whether you're really tough, really brave, or really stupid!" I'd say that I checked the boxes of all three.

There was tension between Lindy and me all season. When I was benched during a game that we won 7–3 in Tampa at the beginning of February 1998, I had had enough. We flew back to Buffalo, and at practice the next day, Lindy and I got into it. The conversation was pretty heated, and I threw a skate through the big-screen TV in the dressing room. I called him a weasel, and he yelled, "What do you want, Barnaby?" I told him, "I want to be traded!" He smashed his stick over my stall and then challenged me. "You wanna fight?" I told him I didn't want to fight him there in the dressing room, but I said, "If you wanna go 15 miles out of town where there is no one around, I will gladly kick the shit out of you!"

This was in front of the whole team. And I still was a Sabre. A lot of stuff went down in Buffalo that was just crazy! We used to say, "Ruff at home, Lindy on the road." It was a slight on his playing career—he'd play tough in front of the home fans, but not when he played on the road.

We had a West Coast road trip at the end of March. With the trade deadline coming up, I brought seven bags full of clothes with me, knowing I was going to be moved, but the trade still didn't happen until a year later.

We finished third in the Northeast. We missed Patty LaFontaine for most of the season (he only played 13 regular-season games in 1997–98), but guys such as Derek Plante and Donald Audette led the team in goals. After a career season, my production was way off, scoring just 5 goals and 25 points. Without Ted Nolan's confidence in me, giving me playing opportunities, my role was pretty much exclusively as a fourth-line agitator. Still, I led Buffalo with 289 minutes in penalties.

The playoffs that year were the best month of my hockey career. I will never, ever forget that spring for a number of amazing reasons. The Sabres faced Philadelphia in the first round of the playoffs. I knew the fans hated me, and I loved it! I started to think of things that would get under the skin of fans even more. Opposing rinks hate guys who are cocky, so I thought I'd have some fun. I had my two front teeth custom-designed in silver with the Sabres logo on each of them. I don't take myself too seriously, so I knew our fans would love it and I knew it would piss off the Philadelphia fans even more. Guys thought it was cocky and called me an idiot, but it was to get under the skin of the other team during that playoff series. I was anxious to give the Philadelphia fans my biggest grin.

I had had my teeth knocked out about five times that season. There was no sense in getting permanent teeth, because if you get in a fight, they're going to get knocked out again. My dentist, Dr. Dan Houston, was a good friend, so I discussed my teeth with him. I said, "Dan, why don't we put the Sabres logo on the front teeth, and I'll wear them through the playoffs?" It made the cover of the *Hockey News*. By the way, it actually hurt. I'm not sure whether the roots of the teeth weren't compatible with the metal or what it was, but even though I thought it would be fun, it wasn't as much fun as I thought.

I first chipped my front tooth in Junior. It was just a chip, so I didn't bother to get it fixed. The first time I got my teeth knocked out was on December 6, 1996, in a game against Anaheim in Buffalo. I went to the net near the end of the game and got crosschecked by Jason Marshall and lost my front six teeth. I had separated my shoulder and had various other injuries, but that was a pain like nothing I had known. All those teeth were jagged and the nerves were exposed.

My dentist tried to freeze my mouth, but it wasn't taking. Dan was not only our dentist, but he lived two doors down from me in the complex where I lived. He and his family were friends of mine. After about 10 freezings, I was snapping! I was in such agony. "Fuckin' freeze me, Dan!" He was drilling, but my mouth wasn't frozen and it hurt like fuck! The pain was excruciating and the adrenaline was pumping, and at one point, I punched Dan right in the stomach! "Fuck! Stop this now! It hurts too much!" We had to jump on a plane and play Hartford the next night. "Dan, ya gotta do something!" He put some kind of putty in my mouth so that the nerve endings wouldn't be exposed.

I got on the plane, but my mouth was still killing me. I could barely eat, so I took small morsels and chewed on my back molars. Teddy Nolan was our coach at the time and asked, "Are you sure you can go?" I told him I was fine to play.

I didn't wear a cage or anything to protect my mouth when we were playing the Whalers. I ended up scoring two goals in the game, but at one point, Stu Grimson and I were in the corner and that motherfucker reached into my mouth and tried to pull the putty stuff right out of my mouth! I was swatting his hands away like I was swatting a bee because I didn't want him near my mouth, it hurt so bad. I don't know whether he knew about my teeth—I was later told he did—but he was trying to get his hands in my mouth!

We were back in Buffalo a few days later. Dr. Dan was able to calm me down and do the root canals that I needed to have done.

I had a good series against the Flyers, silver teeth and all, picking up a goal and four assists as we dumped them four games to one. The final game, May 1, 1998, was a 3–2 overtime win to eliminate the Flyers.

My wife was going to give birth to our first child. We were so excited. I could hardly wait to be a father and give my child the love of a dad that I never had. My son Matthew was born on May 2, 1998; it was awesome to watch him being born. He was perfect. You can't appreciate what true love is until you have a child.

Christine and the baby were in the hospital for a few days after the birth. I would practice with the team and then go over to the hospital to be with Christine and Matthew. I slept there the night before home games, and the nurses really catered to me. I'd get pancakes in the morning before practice during the series against Philadelphia, while poor Christine would have to wait for her breakfast.

I still had a hockey season to continue, and next up were the Canadiens. That series didn't start until May 8, 1998, so I had a few days at home with Christine and Matthew. We had finished the season in sixth place in the conference with 89 points, and Montreal was seventh with 87. We started the series at home and beat Montreal 3–2 on an overtime goal by Geoff Sanderson in Game 1.

I have had a lot of injuries during my NHL career, but the worst I was hurt was in the series against Montreal. I got hit at center ice by Igor Ulanov. He crushed me, really hit me hard. I separated my shoulder. I went to the room and told the trainer I wanted to play, so he gave me a cortisone shot and I went back out. Cortisone shots—best thing ever! You play but don't feel it and take the usual punishment and then ice it down after the game. You go back to the hotel, drink a few beers, hang out with the guys, and talk about the game, and then the next morning, you're in misery and can't move your arm. Back to the rink, another cortisone shot, and you're ready to go again. It was a vicious cycle through that entire playoff. I played through the injury and yet I had my best playoff. Go figure.

Besides my fight with Garth Snow, the other thing I get asked about the most is my game against Montreal on May 10, 1998. It seems appropriate that it was Mother's Day. I was still euphoric but had to focus on hockey. My mother and brother had come down from Ottawa to meet my new baby, and they went to the game that night.

Andy Moog started in goal for Montreal in that second game. I scored late in the second period, and then 13 seconds into the third, I got my second of the night. That's when Moog was pulled in favor of Jocelyn Thibault. I scored my third in the last minute of the game, and we won 6–3. It was the only hat trick I ever scored in the NHL and one of my very few four-point games. I was chosen as the First Star of the Game. I was so happy that my family was there to see the game!

Michael Peca scored in the second overtime of Game 3 for a 5–4 win, and then I scored the opening goal of Game 4 as we finished the sweep with a 3–1 victory.

Buffalo had never gone that deep into the playoffs before, and of course, neither had I. The conference final! We were matched up with Washington. We knew we could beat them.

I picked up an assist on Michael Grosek's goal on the way to a 2–0 win in Game 1 on the road at the MCI Center in Washington. In Game 2 we were down 2–1 late in the third, but I scored an unassisted goal to tie the game and force overtime. Washington scored for a 3–2 win and tied up the series at a game apiece.

We felt good playing in front of our fans in Buffalo for Games 3 and 4, and that also gave me the chance to see Christine and the baby. My goal in the second period of the third game tied the score at two, and it was all tied at three at the end of regulation, so again we went to overtime. And again Washington pulled off a win.

We played well but lost 2–0 in Game 4, so it was back to Washington for Game 5. Jason Woolley scored the deciding goal in a 2–1 Sabres win to keep our hopes alive. We were back in Buffalo for Game 6 and a chance to tie the series. We traded goals in the second and the third, and again we went to overtime, but Joey Juneau ended our season with the overtime winner. Done like fucking dinner!

For a season that was so full of drama and anger, it turned out to be the best season Buffalo had while I was there, and those playoffs were the best hockey I ever played in the NHL. I keep a souvenir of that great playoff framed in my sports room: Yep, my silver teeth with the Sabres logos.

CHAPTER 8

A CHANGE OF SCENERY

I HAD REPEATEDLY ASKED TO BE TRADED. I practically begged. Lindy Ruff and I didn't see eye to eye, and as much as I loved Buffalo, I had to get out. Yet, there I was, attending training camp in 1998, still playing for the Sabres with Lindy Ruff behind the bench and Dominik Hasek in goal. I knew I would eventually be moved, but until that day came, I was still a Sabre. I was playing my role the only way I knew how—skating hard, chirping at the other team, and contributing in any way I could.

By the end of October 1998, we were in last place in the Northeast Division, but we always enjoyed the rivalry we had with Toronto. We hadn't lost at home against the Leafs since 1991. On October 30 at home, in the first of a home-and-home series, I scored and we won 4–1. We knew it was going to be a great game with a lot of intensity, and it was. In the third, Tie Domi and I picked up unsportsmanlike minors, and I picked up a misconduct. The next night, in Toronto, Kris King and I fought in the first period, and then we went again in the second. I picked up two assists in the third period, and we won 6–3.

We had just arrived home after beating Toronto on Halloween night. It was around 12:30 in the morning, and I met my wife, Christine, and her good friend Carla Todaro, whose family was well-known in the Mafia world. The Todaros owned La Nova Pizza in Buffalo. The three of us went over to Chippewa Street for a couple of drinks. The Sabres weren't playing again until November 3. I ended up walking with Christine and Carla, who were all dressed up for Halloween in cute 1960s miniskirts, to House O'Quinn, a bar in the area. The girls were walking ahead of me because I lagged behind while I ate a hot dog. All of a sudden, I saw Christine and Carla being confronted by a group of guys. I heard Carla say, "Say that to me again," and the guy repeated a lewd comment about what he wanted to do to the two girls.

Carla reached up and punched the guy. She grew up in a family that didn't take shit from anyone. I saw this and didn't think twice—I jumped in and started throwing punches. I was hitting the guy while his friends were grabbing me. Next thing I know, one bouncer grabbed me, another one grabbed Christine, and another grabbed Carla and threw the three of us into a police car. "Take care of these three! Get them out of here! We'll take care of the others," one of the bouncers told the cop in the driver's seat.

The officer drove us to the Towne Restaurant, a place where a lot of people in Buffalo went after the bars. We went in, ordered some food, and were laughing away. We couldn't fully understand what had just gone down. It turned out that the bouncers at House O'Quinn knew us because we had partied there before, plus they knew and liked Christine's father, Frank Cardarella, who had been a police officer in Buffalo for 27 years, so they got us out of there.

In the meantime, the cops arrested the guy who had harassed Carla and Christine. You can only imagine the sight—the guy I was punching had been dressed up like Santa Claus for Halloween! And there he was, handcuffed and being thrown into the back of a police cruiser! He was charged with disorderly conduct after he "failed to disperse the area of the fight and did push an officer."

I informed team officials, and there was no disciplinary action. I was more concerned about kids seeing Santa being arrested by the police and ruining their holiday, but it was 3:00 in the morning, so I don't think I had to worry about that too much.

The season continued, but it was almost like the Sword of Damocles hung over my head. I knew I was going to be moved, but I just didn't know when. The Sabres didn't want to trade me, but I wanted out and forced the trade. It was time. I figured I'd be moved at the trade deadline. It took a year and a half. I was rumored to be going to Calgary, Ottawa, Pittsburgh, or Tampa. It wasn't up to me.

The Sabres came to me one last time and said, "You can end this at any point, but if not, we're going to move you." I replied, "No. The time has come. I want to move on." I just wanted to go to a place where I'd fit in, and it ended up being Pittsburgh. On March 11, 1999, I was traded to the Penguins, and Stu Barnes—a really good guy and a great player—went to Buffalo. Barney got traded for Barnesy.

I was excited about joining Pittsburgh, but as much as you think you're ready, it's still a shock when they tell you. My wife was from Buffalo and my son was born in Buffalo. My wife's family was there, so we had built-in babysitters. All of my friends were in Buffalo. I spent seven years of my life—and became a man—in Buffalo. I went from a child with a half-chipped tooth and a mullet to a husband, a father, and an NHL hockey player there.

Being a fan favorite in Buffalo, a city that knows and loves its hockey, was really special. It was very hard to leave, but I'm a confident guy and not someone who's afraid of change, so while I was nervous, I was also very excited.

I walked into my new dressing room, where there were so many great players. It was easy to fit in with the guys in Pittsburgh. They were awesome. I was coming from a really tough team in Buffalo to a skilled team composed largely of European players—Jan Hrdina, Jaromir Jagr, Alex Kovalev, Robert Lang, Alexei Morozov, Jiri Slegr, Martin Straka, Gherman Titov. There were a lot of Europeans, but there really weren't any cliques. The Russian guys stuck together. I mostly hung out with

Kip Miller, Ian Moran, Tyler Wright, and the Czechs. We'd go out for beers together. It was a close-knit, fun group of guys.

Jaromir Jagr was an unbelievable guy. He just loves the game of hockey. I should likely say that he loves life. He wasn't a big drinker, but we'd go out. Jags loved to gamble. He was a little out of control on that side of things. He played blackjack and bet on football. In fact, he'd wager on anything he could bet on. As a teammate, you couldn't find a better guy. And after practice, I'd go to his house and his mom would make us Czech food.

Two weeks before the trade, when I was still suiting up for the Sabres, I had a pushing and shoving match with Tyler Wright, and he bit my fingers through my glove. When I met him in the dressing room as teammates, we just laughed about it. There was no animosity.

Our goalie, Tommy Barrasso, was quite a guy. The word *cocky* doesn't even do him justice. He was the most arrogant person I had ever met. I can laugh about it now. I remember asking Tommy what kind of Ferrari he had brought to the rink one day. He responded, "Don't worry about it, kid. You'll never be able to afford one."

At one of my first practices in Pittsburgh, I took a slap shot from the hash mark, and it went right over his glove and I scored. I celebrated my goal. I was new to the team and was just being myself. I was laughing and high-fiving. He charged out of his crease and blurted, "How many Hart Trophies have you won?" I said, "None." He asked, "How many Stanley Cups have you won?" I said, "None." He said, "That's right! Only 66 and 68 shoot hard top-glove slap shots on me! You keep it low!"

Tommy's not a bad guy. We coexisted just fine. He just lives a different life than I do. He has to drink the finest wines, drive the nicest cars. Tommy is Tommy, and you're never changing Tommy. If you ever want to know how good a goalie Tommy Barrasso is, just ask Tommy.

Going to Pittsburgh was definitely an eye-opening experience. I expected to walk into Pittsburgh playing the same role I had in Buffalo, but I was cast in a fourth-line role with the Penguins, and there were nights when I hardly got a shift. But the real problem was that I went from fighting a heavyweight once in a while to fighting the opponents' toughest guys every night. I went from a team in Buffalo that had Rob Ray, Brad May, and Bob Boughner—they were the heavyweights. In Buffalo I could choose the fights that I wanted—whether I wanted to fight the heavyweights. In Pittsburgh I was the *only* guy who fought, and I *had* to fight the heavyweights. When things started to go awry or the team needed a jolt, I had to fight Stu Grimson, Darren McCarty, Bob Probert, or any one of the heavyweights across the league. I hadn't realized how much I appreciated the heavyweights on the Sabres. I wasn't a heavyweight, but in Pittsburgh, I was cast in that role. And they also expected me to chip in with 15 goals every season.

It's a lot different preparing for a game when you know you're going to have to fight. I never had to think about that in Buffalo; I just thought about playing hockey. If a fight occurred or if the team needed a jolt, I could be that guy, but when I went to Pittsburgh, if anything rough went on in the game, I was expected to fight the toughest guy on their team. Some of those guys were 6'5" and 240 pounds. I was six feet tall and weighed 180 pounds. It was a hard, hard way to play. We were a team full of Europeans who didn't really fight, so my game suffered.

The Penguins were coached by Kevin Constantine. I didn't know anything about him, but immediately I could tell that I didn't fit in to the way he wanted the team to play. He absolutely hated the way that I played. I started thinking, *Holy shit! I've got myself into a situation where the coach doesn't like what I do.* He had really liked Stu Barnes's game. I didn't play much. We didn't butt heads, but we never really talked.

Constantine was an arrogant son of a bitch. He was a bad guy. No one wants to get a coach fired, especially because of losses. Players are proud, and they do not want to lose—and no one plays poorly to get a coach fired. But I can tell you that there were many nights in the back of the bus when the conversation was, "If we lose tomorrow, this fucker is gone!"

Video is good, but I've never seen a guy break down video like Constantine. I've seen him break down video with Jaromir Jagr, trying to correct Jaromir from turning the wrong way. Jagr just laughed at him as though he were saying, "This guy's got no fucking clue." Having said that, Constantine was the smartest hockey coach I've ever seen with X's and O's. He would have rather coached robots, which I certainly wasn't. He's just not a good dude.

The Pittsburgh market is very much like Buffalo. Right away, because of the way I played, I became a fan favorite. The Pittsburgh fans appreciated what I did. I scored a couple of goals in March after the trade, even though I didn't play a lot. You never want the guy you got traded for to make you look bad, and Stu Barnes didn't score for Buffalo in the regular season after the trade, although he did catch fire in the playoffs and contributed to Buffalo's magic run. It's human nature to want the guy you got traded for not to do well.

After I got traded, I circled March 27, 1999, on the calendar—the first time we'd playing against the Buffalo Sabres. I really looked forward to playing that game.

It was really weird going back to Buffalo as a visitor for the first time. I had been loved by the fans in Buffalo. At the rink that night, I took a good look around at the seats. I saw signs—WE LOVE YOU, BAM BAM and MATT'S A RAT—stuff like that. The fans were looking forward to my return. Six minutes into the first period, I scored on a two-on-one with Rob Brown against Dominik Hasek. I went nuts and skated by the Buffalo bench, laughing at Lindy Ruff. There is nothing you love more than to fuck your former team.

The night before the game, Rob Ray came over to the house that I kept in Buffalo. My wife made spaghetti and we had a couple bottles of wine. Rob warned me, "Don't be a fucking idiot tomorrow." I told him I was coming back and had to play my game. Coming back in the opponents' jersey, I was the villain now. "I know, I know," Rob said. "Just don't start running around and hitting guys."

I played my game. I was chirping at Lindy Ruff on the bench, calling him every name in the book, and I was banging and crashing into my former teammates. I was digging into some of the guys I didn't care for as much, telling them to stop sucking Lindy's cock. Rob came over to me and said, "Bud, you gotta slow down! Lindy sent me out to get ya!" I just chuckled and replied, "Rob, you know me. I'm not stoppin', man!"

The puck was along the boards, and Rob hit me. We got into a verbal match and I chopped him on the shoulder. He retaliated and we got into a Zorro battle. We dropped the gloves. Rob is tougher than I am, but it was a pretty even scrap. I was never afraid of Rob even though he was stronger than me. We ended up grappling a little bit. The crowd was going nuts! Rob always fought right, so I really tried to tie up that hand, but he got in a couple of good shots. He was so mad, and of course he had to beat me in front of his home crowd. At the end, I know I had him tied up and he couldn't get a punch in. The linesmen were both in there trying to hold us, and I started laughing at Rob. Big smile. He was so angry! He was fuckin' screaming at me. I don't even know what he was saying because I was laughing, which made him crazier. I got kicked out of the period, so I raised my hands and waved to the crowd. I was getting cheered by some as I was going off and booed by others, but the sound was deafening.

I kept my eye on how the Sabres were doing. Both Buffalo and Pittsburgh were in the Eastern Conference, and we both made the playoffs. They finished with 91 points and we had 90. The Penguins beat New Jersey in the first round in seven games, and Buffalo swept Ottawa. We ended up losing to Toronto four games to two in the conference semifinals. Buffalo went on to beat Boston in the conference semifinals and then Toronto in the conference Final, and then went to the Stanley Cup Final against Dallas.

There I was, a lifelong Sabre, and a couple months after I was traded, Buffalo was playing for the Stanley Cup! I couldn't fucking believe it! All I could think about was that they might win the Stanley Cup and be walking around with rings, something I had dreamed about. I can't lie—I cheered for Buffalo to lose every fucking game! No one says it publicly, but we all think it. I say it.

I was at Game 6 on June 19, sitting in a box with Brad May, who by then had been traded to Vancouver. We were there to watch Brett Hull score in the third overtime to win the Stanley Cup. You could have heard a pin drop except for Brad May and me whooping it up and dancing around in the box! We were drunk and high-fiving!

After the game, we went to a bar called Elmo's, where we knew the guys would be drowning their sorrows. Brad and I were partying while our former teammates were distraught. Brad and I drank until 7:00 the next morning and then walked a few miles over to the Transit Valley Country Club, my golf course. We were drinking Captain Morgan rum and Cokes out of water pitchers.

Brad hadn't asked to be traded when he was dealt to the Canucks. I couldn't imagine having to live with the fact that I had *asked* for a trade and taken myself out of a place that won the Stanley Cup. I loved my teammates in Buffalo and I loved the fans, but it was tough for me. It would've destroyed me if they'd won.

Kevin Constantine called me and told me that I missed my exit interview at the end of the season. I was already home in Buffalo with my wife's family by then. He asked me why I hadn't come in. I said, "Kevin, you think I'm a shitty hockey player. I think you're a shitty coach. What else is there to say?"

* * *

There were rumors floating around about the Penguins franchise moving to Portland, Oregon, or even folding. A US bankruptcy court awarded the ownership to Mario Lemieux, which was really cool. A player owning a team was really a different scenario.

I was back with Pittsburgh for the 1999–2000 season, and so was Kevin Constantine. I knew it was going to be more of the same, but after 24 games, the Penguins fired Kevin and brought in Herb Brooks. What a tremendous man! I didn't know much about the Miracle on Ice because in 1980, NHL players couldn't participate in the Olympics, and my interest was in the NHL and Stanley Cup. After a couple of days, Herb brought me into the office and we had a great talk. He loved me as both a player and a person, and he played me a ton.

Herb hadn't coached in the NHL since 1993 and was a bit out of his element. I came into the dressing room one day that season and I had an *A* on my jersey. I was always the first player at the rink, so I went into the trainer's office and asked him why I was wearing the *A* for alternate captain. He told me that was what the coach wanted. I walked into Herb's office and said, "You can't put that *A* on my jersey." He asked me why not, and I said, "We've got Jagr, Straka, Slegr, and Lang—all great guys and great players, and they're the leaders on the club." Herb fired back, "You're a great leader, Matthew!"

I told him I really appreciated such an honor but I couldn't take an *A* off one of those guys, but he replied that I was more of a leader than those players. I said, "You're going to alienate me from the team! They're going to hate me!" He just shrugged and said, "You're getting an *A*." He decided that he'd add an *A* to the team and I would wear it occasionally, but more importantly to me, Herb believed in me. He played me a ton and was a tremendous man. He confided in me a lot.

We were playing Carolina on December 15, 1999, and I fought Byron Ritchie. We went toe to toe on a faceoff and had a really even fight, punching each other in the face nonstop. We each got in about 15 great punches to the face. I skated off and raised my arms in victory.

We got on the plane after the game, and I was having a few beers. About halfway home, I felt like I was coming down with the flu. When

I got home, I wasn't feeling great. The next morning, I went to the Southpointe rink for practice. I was getting dressed, and I told the trainer I really didn't feel well and that I thought I had the flu. He gave me Advil and told me to go home and to take things easy for the game the next day.

I started to drive home, but I had to pull over. I couldn't remember the route! I had made the trip so many times. I called my wife and told her, "I'm parked at the school. I don't know the name of it and I don't know how to get home." She came and picked me up and we went home. I felt sick and had the worst migraine, and for the next three months, I couldn't stand being in the light, and even everyday noises hurt. My son was just being a normal kid, but I got really irritable with him. I started to get depressed. I failed my concussion test three or four times and even tried to cheat in order to get back in the lineup. There were days when I laid on the floor and sobbed. I was afraid that my career was over.

About a month or two after the fight, I was at lunch with some of the guys and was having some beers. I didn't know that you're not supposed to drink with a concussion. I was talking gibberish. The guys made me call my wife, and she came to get me again.

That was the longest I had been out of the lineup and was the worst injury I had suffered playing hockey. I wasn't in pain, but my head needed to heal. When the doctors finally cleared me to play, I was more than anxious to get back into the lineup. My first game back was against Detroit on January 2, 2000. Although I knew I wasn't 100 percent, I played about 13 minutes, which was usual for me. I was back.

Then on January 13, 2000, we were in Colorado. I had clipped Patrick Roy, and Alexei Gusarov nailed me on the back of the neck. I was down on the ice, and as it turned out, I had another concussion.

The television play-by-play guy for the Avalanche, John Kelly, said I was faking and that I was known for exaggerating injuries. I get it. I was always trying to draw opponents into penalties. I guess I was the boy who cried wolf, but this time I was actually injured. Herb Brooks was told about the remark and went berserk, confronting Kelly after the game. He told him it was a bullshit thing to say and then shoved Kelly. "I'll kick your butt all over the place," he said before a security officer separated them. "Gusarov almost tore his head off, and you say Barnaby has a tendency to embellish!"

Herb was suspended for two games but issued a statement through the team: "Look at the tape. He tore his head off. We have two referees, and they can't find that? Barnaby is just coming off a concussion. He was flat-out—knocked out—and the referees didn't see it. I'm disappointed. I have a responsibility to the organization. What happened was an emotional moment in response to something that happened. I took exception to the disparaging remark made about one of our players. I guess I stood up for the players and our team in the wrong manner. I fully realize that two wrongs don't make a right."

Two days later, before a game against Nashville that he'd miss, Herb called me in my hotel room at 4:00. "What are you doing, Barney?" I told him I was going to get a bite to eat and then head over to the game. "What do you say we meet for a beer?" he asked. I had a concussion, but we didn't have the protocols then that are in place today. We went down to the corner bar and had a few beers and then walked over to the rink together.

For Herbie to stand up for me like that, to show that kind of respect for me, I would do anything for him after that. It was amazing. It gives me chills just thinking about it. And I'm sure that was true of a lot of guys who played for him over the years. Herb Brooks was just a tremendous man.

We were in Calgary on March 1, 2000, and got waxed 8–2. After the game, we had to fly to Edmonton and had a practice there the next day. A practice was the last thing we wanted after the debacle in Calgary. It was a short flight, but the coaches imposed a curfew on us when we arrived. It was 11:30 with no game the next night. Fuck that! The word spread: "In the lobby in 10," which just meant that everybody was to show up and we'd figure out our plan. We actually met outside around the side of the hotel so the coaches wouldn't see us. There were 12 or 13 guys who showed up, so we scurried away so we wouldn't get caught breaking curfew and went to several bars. We stayed out until about 6:00 in the morning even though our practice was at 10!

We were all messes when we showed up at the rink, but we battled through. Eddie Johnston was running the practice, and after we skated, we were stretching. He said, "Okay, boys, you look as hungover as I am. Get some rest, and we'll see you tomorrow for the game." We had to laugh. Eddie was a good guy.

We finished third in the Atlantic Division with 88 points and faced the Washington Capitals in the first round of the playoffs. They had finished with 102 points, so we had our work cut out for us. Then, in the first game, we blanked them 7–0. Holy shit! We ended up winning the series four games to one.

In the conference semifinal, we took the first two games on the road in Philadelphia, and then they came back and beat us in both games in Pittsburgh, both in overtime. Game 4 on May 4, 2000, went to a fifth overtime before the Flyers scored to win the game 2–1. It took seven hours from the opening faceoff until the deciding goal! It was on my birthday, and it was one of the most grueling things I've ever been involved in. The Flyers then won the next two games to end our season.

* * *

The next year, the Penguins thought it was a good idea to bring in Ivan Hlinka to coach the team. He was a great guy who grew up playing and coaching in Czechoslovakia, and the team had seven or eight Czechs on the team, so he was the right guy for them. Ivan liked me as a person, but I didn't fit in to his vision of how the Penguins should play. He didn't play me a lot.

We started the 2000–01 season playing two games against the Nashville Predators in Japan. What an experience that was! We were on the plane heading to Japan for nine days, and one of my teammates walked up and down the aisle of the plane with a small basket asking for everyone's wedding rings! We put our rings in the basket and joked around that while we were in Japan, we were single guys.

While we were there, we went to a bar and were dancing and drinking and carrying on, and one of the players took a picture of us. Another guy grabbed the camera and smashed it on the ground, then handed him $200 and said, "Get yourself a new camera." No one wanted evidence of our shenanigans. Japan was an insane party!

On our off-days, we frequented this one bar in particular. Craig Patrick, our general manager, went in one day and the woman asked what he was doing in Japan. He told her his hockey team was playing in Japan at that time. She looked at him and said, "I hope you're with Nashville because the Pittsburgh Penguins boys have been in here every night until about 4:00 in the morning!" When we were getting dressed for the game that night, Craig came in, looked around the room, and said, "You guys better fuckin' win tonight!" Enter Jaromir Jagr. It's nice to have a superstar on your side.

If there was an Academy Award for Best Portrayal of a Loving Husband, I think I would have received it. After our games in Japan, I came off the plane crying, and my wife asked, "What's with you?" I told her I had missed her so much. She said, "You've been away for 10 days in Japan! Don't give me that bullshit!" What she didn't know was that one of our teammates had passed around a sliced onion to make sure we all had tears in our eyes when we arrived!

Mario Lemieux had retired after the 1996–97 season. He had beaten Hodgkin's lymphoma but had ongoing back ailments. He had already been inducted into the Hockey Hall of Fame, and in September 1999 he became the first NHL player to become the majority owner of his former team. He was president, chairman, and CEO of the Penguins.

In December 2000 we began hearing rumblings that Mario was going to come back, but we were told not to ask about it. He had been retired for three and a half seasons! It would be insane! The rumblings got more prominent, and we heard that he was practicing at a rink with Jay Caufield. Then it was announced to our team before it went to the media that Mario was coming back to play. At the press conference, he said that one of the reasons he was making a return was because his son Austin, who was four, wanted to see his daddy play.

Mario came out and skated with us, and one time during practice, he said, "Hey, Barney, I want you to bump me," and then he'd take the puck to the net. I thought, *I'm not bumping Mario Lemieux!* He was a big man—6'5"—so I wasn't going to hurt him, but what if I bumped him and he rolled an ankle or something? I'd have been traded away from Pittsburgh so quickly! He asked me, but I said, "No thank you! Get a rookie to bump you."

Right before he came back, there were about seven of us out the night before a game, and we had a couple bottles of wine with dinner. Mario was with us. About a quarter to 11:00, I got up and said I was going home. Mario said, "Where are you going? You're with the owner. You're all good here. Sit down." I laughed, sat down, and had a couple more glasses of wine.

Mario's first game back was at home on December 27, 2000, against Toronto. He picked up an assist on his first shift and finished with a goal and two assists, and we won 5–0. I was suspended for that game, so I was up in the stands watching, thinking, *This is fucking insane!* He scored 35 goals and had 76 points in the 43 games he played that season!

There was no arrogance or cockiness with Mario. He may have been the owner of the team and one of the greatest players ever to play, but he carried himself as just another player on the team. He loved to have fun. Mario is a great, great guy.

Ivan Hlinka, our coach, didn't speak a lot of English and didn't appreciate the way that I played. The beginning of the end was

January 21, 2001, in Chicago. I hadn't played a fucking shift all night. I was sitting on the end of the bench chirping at Bob Probert and Ryan VandenBussche, telling them they were pieces of shit, calling their mothers and their wives every obscenity you can dream of. I had one personal rule: no kids and no dogs, but wives, girlfriends, and mothers were fair game. I yelled from the bench all game long.

We were up 4–0, and with about three minutes to go, Chicago put all their tough guys on. Ivan looked down the bench and yelled, "Barney! You're up!" My skates were untied. I looked over at him and shouted back, "Ivan! Fuck you!"

"Barney! You're up!"

"No, I'm not!" It would have taken a fucking crane to get me onto the ice at that point. There was no fucking chance I was going over the boards. I would have been ripped to shreds by the Hawks' tough guys. I was freezing cold on the bench with my skates untied, and they would have killed me for all the things that I'd said.

I called over Randy Hillier, our assistant coach. I said, "Randy, explain the situation to Ivan. I am not—I repeat, *not*—going out on the ice." Randy nodded and talked to Ivan. I didn't play a shift that game, and I remember talking to Craig Patrick after the game. He was a guy I absolutely loved. He respected me. I told him, "Ivan's a great guy, but he doesn't appreciate the way I play and what I bring to the table. If you can find a trade partner for me, I think it would be best that I find an opportunity to play somewhere else."

After the game, I went to see Craig Patrick, our GM. I said, "Craig, you're a great guy. Ivan's a great guy. I love the team and appreciate everything you've done for me, but it's obvious that I don't fit in to the team that Ivan needs and wants. Would you mind moving me?" Craig said he totally understood, and a few weeks later, over the 2001 All-Star break, he traded me to the Tampa Bay Lightning.

I had been a fan favorite in Pittsburgh. We had the Barnaby Brigade there. When I skated out onto the ice to start a game, or if I got a penalty, they played a video clip accompanied by the song "Born to Be Wild." It was crazy! I loved Pittsburgh, but I had to make a change. All I could think about was providing for my family and making as much money as I could.

I loved the fans in Pittsburgh. They were incredible. I loved the players who I played with. They were awesome. Despite the fact that the team had a lot of European players, it was a very close team. We had modest success.

In Pittsburgh I had one coach who liked me in Herb Brooks, one who hated me in Kevin Constantine, and one who liked me but didn't know how to use me in Ivan Hlinka. I was exactly the same player for all three coaches. Coaches can make or break you.

CHAPTER 9

NEVER SETTLE

I HADN'T BEEN PLAYING A LOT IN PITTSBURGH, so on February 1, 2001, Craig Patrick traded me to Tampa Bay. It was the Penguins' fifth trade in two weeks. I was excited about going to Tampa because it would give me a chance to play with a buddy of mine, Wayne Primeau. Then I found out he was the guy going to Pittsburgh in the trade!

The Lightning were already out of the playoffs by the time I got there. John Tortorella was the Lightning's coach. I knew Torts a little bit because he had been an assistant coach in Buffalo during my first couple of years there. Tortorella was a really great coach, although he could be an asshole at the rink. He had the toughest practices, but away from the rink, he was one of the nicest guys you'd ever want to meet. He really cared for his players.

John was very honest with me up front. He pulled me aside one day and said, "I don't think you skate well enough to be able to play a lot with the Lightning." I was the only fighter on the team, so again I was forced to fight all the heavyweights all the time. I was only playing seven or eight minutes a game. There is no way you can have offensive success with so few minutes of playing time. You get on the ice, you're fighting the toughest guy on the opposing team, you get beat up, and it's done.

I ended up leading the league in penalty minutes again in 2000–01. I had led the league in that category in 1995–96 with Buffalo when I had 335 minutes in penalties, and when the league combined my 168 penalty minutes with Pittsburgh and 97 with Tampa, I led the league that season with 265.

At the end of the season, we had exit meetings. I was a free agent, but I wanted to come back. We were negotiating my contract, and my agent, Larry Kelly, called me. He told me, "They've just offered you $4.5 million over three years." I was already making $1.1 million, so I was excited, but Larry said, "With your stats, this is not going to be a popular signing. We have to get this signed right now."

Larry drove to Watertown, New York, which was about two hours from where he lived, and my buddy Don Arthur and I jumped into my car, drove three hours, and met Larry on the side of the highway. We signed the contract at 10:00 at night in order to get it done. Larry was afraid they were going to pull the offer once other GMs found out what it was. If you think that there's not collusion, you're wrong.

I went to training camp in great shape. I had worked out super hard that summer. I figured with a three-year deal at that money, I was going to play a lot. It turned out that wasn't the case.

The group in Tampa wasn't particularly close-knit. It was a younger team, but the guys were awesome. Nikolai Khabibulin was an unbelievable goalie. He worked his ass off. I loved Vinny Lecavalier and Brad Richards. They were cocky kids but great guys and great players. I don't mind cocky. They were the core of that team that went on to win the Stanley Cup in 2004. The guy who stood out to me was Marty St. Louis. You can't find a better guy or a harder worker, and his commitment on and off the ice was unparalleled. He had been drafted by Calgary, cut, and told he was too small, and look at what he did! He's someone for people to look up to. I watched him every day, and I knew he was going to be a star. There was no way he was going to be denied. He was one of the best players I ever played with.

The leader was clearly Dave Andreychuk, one of the veterans, who was with Buffalo in 1992–93 when I got called up at the end of the season for my first NHL games. He's an unbelievable guy. We were going out every night before a game. We weren't breaking curfew, but we liked to hang out together. Dave loves to tip them back. There aren't many guys who can drink as many beers in a sitting as Dave. He's an absolute machine! I challenged him one night at a Red Robin in New Jersey. He buried me in two hours! We both had 8 beers, and I looked up and Tim Taylor said, "Just wait!" I had 9.5, and Andy was at 14 and still going strong. Dave is a great, great guy—a Hall of Famer on the ice and off.

I wasn't playing very much, so I asked Torts if I could talk to him. He said sure. I wondered why I wasn't getting much ice time, and he told me that he didn't think I was good enough to help the team. He was very honest, and I appreciated that. I didn't like hearing that, but I appreciated it. I told him that if that was the case and I wasn't going to play, I'd ask Jay Feaster, the GM, to trade me.

Everybody thinks I'm crazy, but every move is well calculated. I like two things—to make money and to be in a great situation. The money is so I can set up my kids in a good situation so they don't have to struggle. The money in Tampa was great, but if I wasn't wanted, I had to go.

I had signed a three-year contract for $1.5 million a year with Tampa. I had just finished building my dream house and I had to come home and tell my wife that I had asked to be traded. We had only lived in the house for 10 days. That was a tough discussion! I told my wife, "This is what we have to do. If not, this lifestyle is going to end very quickly."

My wife trusted my instincts. I've put a lot of thought into everything I've ever done. I've certainly made mistakes, but when it came to business decisions, I didn't make them without a lot of thought. I knew if I didn't get out of Tampa Bay, my career was going to be over.

I sat down with Jay Feaster, and he agreed to find a deal for me. He found a partner in the New York Rangers, and on December 12, 2001, Zdeno Ciger went to the Lightning and I was off to Broadway.

*   *   *

It was a great trade for me. I wasn't the heavyweight, so I didn't have to fight every night, and I had coaches who believed in me again. Our general manager was Glen Sather, and I love Glen for trading for me. I went from laid-back Tampa, where you wear your flip-flops to the rink, to the lights and glamour of New York City. While playing for different teams, I had spent a few nights in New York, but playing there was unlike anything I'd ever experienced. I was living in the Southpoint Hotel, right across from Madison Square Garden. I would step out of the hotel and walk to Madison Square Garden. Our practices were at the PlayLand Ice Casino in Rye, New York, and I'd get a ride there.

I played a lot—13 or 14 minutes per night. After a couple of years of really struggling to find a spot where I fit and with a coach who believed in me, New York was a career changer for me. I had three of the most successful seasons of my career.

I looked around the room: Brian Leetch, Mark Messier, Petr Nedved, Vladimir Malakhov, Mike Richter, Bryan Berard, Theo Fleury. Our payroll was around $90 million in 2001! I remember thinking, *Wow! We're winning a Stanley Cup!* But I was with the Rangers for three years, and we never made the playoffs!

I was thrown onto a line with Petr Nedved and Radek Dvorak, and I played regularly. I was playing third-line minutes every night, and I was scoring. Plus, I didn't have to be the heavyweight anymore! We had Sandy McCarthy and Dale Purinton. I had fought Dale a few months earlier when I was in Tampa. Nothing really happened, but at the end of the fight, he said, "Guns N' Roses rule!" When I walked into the room, I thought, *This guy is wacko*, but he came up to me, gave me a hug, and said, "Love your game! We're teammates now. I got your back!" It's always good to have a guy who's got your back. Dale had his name tattooed in a name bar on his!

I don't get impressed meeting anyone, but when I walked into the room, I was nervous meeting Mark Messier. He was bigger than life and had an aura around him. I grew up watching the Oilers during their Stanley Cup years, and now I was going to have a chance to play with Mess.

Most of the shit I said to Eric Lindros through the years can't be repeated. I chirped at him about his mother all the time, things such as, "Mommy let you play tonight, E-tard?" I ripped him for years. I walked into the dressing room, and there he was. We just looked at each other and started laughing. And wouldn't you know, we became roommates. I love the guy.

I would say that Eric is misunderstood. He was placed on a pedestal from the time he was about eight years old. If I were going to build a hockey player from scratch, it would be Eric Lindros. Eric could have played in any era—the 1960s, '70s, '80s, or '90s. He'd be unstoppable today. He was 6'5" and 250 pounds, skated like the wind, and hit like a Mack truck. The battles we had when I was in Buffalo and he was with Philadelphia were insane. I called him every name in the book. He kicked my legs out.

Eric was a really generous guy—good teammate, great roommate. We had a lot of laughs. He was so good to my kids when they'd visit the dressing room. He'd pull on the pads and let my son Matthew fire shots at him. At Halloween he'd take my daughter and put her on the back of his dog, Bacchus, to go trick-or-treating. He was always looking out for the trainers too. When guys were called up from the minors, he'd get a group of us together at his house to welcome them to the team. The animosity he faced goes back to his parents. They were a little overbearing. They seemed to believe there was some conspiracy against Eric, but the team was paying him a ton of money. They wanted success.

On November 11, 2002, we were in San Jose staying at the Fairmont Hotel. We were going to fly out the next day. There were a bunch of guys in our room playing poker, and we ordered about 50 beers from room service. There were room service trays everywhere. At some point, Eric and I started wrestling, just having fun, and then Sandy McCarthy and Rem Murray joined in. Before you know it, everybody was wrestling and we had destroyed the room. When we woke up the next morning, Eric and I looked around and knew we were in trouble. We went down to the front desk and spoke with the manager and told him that our room was a disaster—broken lights, broken beds, you name it. Eric and I gave the manager our credit cards and told him to total up the damage and then split the cost over the two cards. We told him how sorry we were and that things had gotten out of hand. "Mr. Barnaby and Mr. Lindros—I'll take care of it," the manager said. Eric and I figured that we were both in for about $5,000.

About a month went by, Glen Sather, our general manager, called us into his office after practice. We wondered, *What the fuck could this be about?* We never thought about San Jose. That was done and dusted. We walked into Glen's office, and there had to have been 40 Polaroid pictures of our room on his desk. He had his feet on the desk and a cigar in his mouth, and he leaned forward. "What the fuck happened in San Jose? I understand that you guys were drinking, but what the fuck were you guys doing?" We told him we were just playing cards and having drinks.

Glen had traded Rem Murray two hours earlier. Eric and I looked at each other and, in unison, said, "It was Rem Murray." Glen just looked at us, then said, "I coached the Oilers in the 1980s, and that team partied harder than any team that ever played! One time an entire hotel floor was flooded, but I never heard about it! Get the fuck out of my office!" The next paychecks Eric and I got from the Rangers were a lot lighter; they billed us for the damage. We were stunned that Sather knew, let alone that we had to reimburse the hotel at that point. We thought we had done that!

Glen Sather looked at the free agents available, and whoever was the best, he went out and got them. In March 2002 he picked up Pavel Bure, but Pavel was at the end of his career. Before the 2002–03 season, he signed Bobby Holik. We were sitting on the bench in practice one day working on our power play and penalty-killing, and Bobby said, "Barney! Did Sather not watch me play for the last 10 years?" Bobby Holik was a really good player, but he was not a first-line center. In New Jersey he had established himself as a hardworking, dependable shutdown guy. If Bobby Holik was our third-line center, a penalty killer, and maybe on our second power-play unit, we would win a Stanley Cup. But if Bobby Holik was our first-line center and on the first power-play unit, we wouldn't make the fucking playoffs. Bobby Holik was one of the greatest teammates I ever had—a great, honest guy. It was all about winning with Bobby.

In January 2004 Sather picked up Jaromir Jagr. I love Jags. I played with him in Pittsburgh.

The Rangers were the most cliquey team I played for. Part of it was that we had so many stars on the team, but much of it was the dynamic of living in New York. Some guys lived outside the city and some lived in the city. We were pretty spread out. After games, guys who lived in the city would go to certain restaurants, the single guys would hang out, and the guys who lived outside the city would head home. Plus we had a lot of "big" guys. What I mean is that Petr Nedved was going out with a different model every night, Mark Messier was going out with his friends somewhere else, and so on.

Brian Leetch is the most humble superstar I've ever met in my life. He was quiet but funny, and he played hard every shift. Brian was a great teammate and a pleasure to play with. He'd never talk about himself, but he is one of the greatest defensemen who ever played the game. I just respect Brian so much.

Bryan Berard was awesome. We only played together in the 2001–02 season. I fought Bryan early in our careers, but I have so much respect for him. Bryan got clipped in the right eye while playing with Toronto in March 2000. A stick severely slashed his eye. He missed the rest of that season and underwent seven eye operations. They saved his eye, but his sight in that eye was minimal. The insurance company game him a $6.5 million settlement, but he was determined to play hockey again. When his sight had returned to the league minimum, he gave back that insurance money and signed a tryout contract with the Rangers. Bryan played well enough that they signed him to a contract. Bryan is a tremendous human being. He was so fun to be with, and we loved him as a teammate. We're pretty similar in many ways: He likes to get after it and party, and I like to get after it and party too.

The Mark Messier I got to know was different from the Mark Messier of the Oilers in the 1980s. Mark was 39 years old and nearing the end of his career when he returned to the Rangers in 2000–01. His preparation was incredible. He was the captain but not a rah-rah guy in the room; when he spoke, you listened. When we played on the same line, I always had his back and he always had mine. I look back at playing with Mess, one of the best players of all time, and the privilege that it was.

We went through so many coaches. When I got to New York, we had Ron Low. He was old school and an awesome guy. I was skating around one day at practice and my nose started bleeding. I was staying in a hotel at the time, and it was dry. He yelled over, "Lay off the coke, Barnaby!" I let it go at practice, but I was riled up. I love to party, but I have never done a drug in my life. I know on the ice I have the persona of being a wild man, but I have never even smoked a joint, let alone done cocaine. After the practice, I went to the coach's office and I was fuming. I asked Ron, "Why the fuck would you say that?" He told me he was just joking around, but I told him, "I don't want anybody thinking I do coke! That's how rumors get started!"

The next year we started with Bryan Trottier, and when he was fired, Glen Sather took over. In 2003–04 we had Tom Renney, one of the best and smartest coaches I ever had and one of the finest people I ever met.

Our team just never made the playoffs while I was there. There would have been no better place to win a Stanley Cup than in New

York. The Rangers are the pinnacle of teams in the National Hockey League. It's hard to comprehend why things didn't work. We had too many great players. You can't build an All-Star team. Every player has to feel really comfortable in their role. On most teams, you have your top six forwards to provide offense, a checking line, and back then you had a fourth line of tough guys. When you have three lines with every player thinking they should be on the first line, there just isn't enough ice time to go around, so nobody's happy. Every player bases their season on statistics, so if you're used to playing on the first line but are relegated to third-line minutes, you're not happy. We had a lot of stars but didn't have enough role players.

The Rangers were headed for a seventh straight year of missing the playoffs. I was very popular in New York and had three of my best years in the league there, but we couldn't get it done. I knew I was going to get traded because I was an unrestricted free agent. I loved playing in New York, but the team underachieved.

Glen Sather unloaded 10 of us in 7 days at the trade deadline in March 2004, picking up 15 players and 6 draft picks. Gone were Greg de Vries, Paul Healey, Alex Kovalev, Brian Leetch, Vladimir Malakhov, Jussi Markannen, Petr Nedved, Martin Rucinsky, Chris Simon, and me.

The writing was on the wall during the last six weeks I was in New York. I was just waiting and hearing rumors that I might be going to Boston, Toronto, or Ottawa. Then all of a sudden, Colorado started popping up.

I used to take the trainers out for dinner when we were on the road to thank them for all the things they did. It was March 3, 2004, and while I was sitting there with the Rangers trainers, we had the Vancouver-Colorado game on the TV. This was only a couple of days before the trade deadline so I asked our public relations guy, Darren Blake, where I was going. He said, "I don't know. I hear the same rumors you're hearing."

We stopped eating for a few moments to watch a fight between Brad May of the Canucks and Peter Worrell of Colorado while Steve Moore of the Avalanche fought Matt Cooke. It was a wild game, and that was the night of the Todd Bertuzzi incident with Steve Moore.

Just then Darren said, "You're going to be receiving a call in a couple of minutes." I begged him, "Who the fuck is it?" My heart was pumping. I was excited. I was anxious. I wanted to tell my family where we were going. Darren was laughing, and just then, my phone rang. It was Pierre Lacroix, the GM of the Avalanche. We only played a couple of times a year in the Western Conference, so I didn't know much about the Avalanche, but I knew who was in their lineup, and I was excited. The Avalanche were going for it and made seven trades before the deadline that season. In addition to me, they also picked up Bob Boughner, Chris Gratton, Darby Henrickson, Tommy Salo, Kurt Sauer, and Ossi Vaananen.

I remember walking into the conference room when we were in Edmonton to play the Oilers on March 10. Tony Granato was the coach and Rick Tocchet and Jacques Cloutier were the assistant coaches. They said, "Look around. This is our team. We're going for it! We're going to win this year!" I looked around. Joe Sakic, Peter Forsberg, Paul Kariya, Adam Foote, and Teemu Selanne. I was 12 years into my career, and I was excited: "We're winning a Stanley Cup!"

The guys were awesome! I loved my time in New York, but the attitude in the room with Colorado was so different. It was always about "team." The three hardest workers on the team were Joe Sakic, Peter Forsberg, and Paul Kariya. There was nowhere else to go but to follow the leaders. Teemu Selanne was my roommate on the road. I was surprised that there were no cliques on this team. This was a team that didn't go out and party. We'd check in to a hotel and get together to play poker—not with big stakes. Everyone was treated as an equal. We had fun. Adam Foote would be on our plane and hold Paul Kariya down and tickle him. Paul would giggle like a little girl, and we would all laugh so hard!

I mostly hung out with Rob Blake, Bob Boughner, Jim Cummins, and Adam Foote, but everyone got along so well. Chris Gratton and I hated each other when we played against each other earlier in our careers. We fought, and the things I said to him were brutal. But he was my center and lived in the same building as me, and we became very good friends.

I loved playing for Colorado. It is one of my favorite places. I was not the heavyweight there. We had Bob Boughner, Jim Cummins, and Peter Worrell, so I didn't have to fight. I could play my game, mix it up, and pick my spots. I slid into a role on the third line right away and had four goals and five assists in the 13 regular-season games left in the season.

The big rivalry the Avalanche had was with Detroit. There was bad blood going back to May 1996 when Claude Lemieux hit Kris Draper from behind, breaking his jaw, nose, and cheekbone and causing a concussion. This sparked a fierce rivalry between the teams. The hatred was still there when we played.

On March 25, 2004, Darren McCarty of the Red Wings and I were lining up. I said, "D-Mac, let's go, bud!" I was archenemy number one in Colorado, and we went toe to toe. Darren was a lefty, and that always catches guys off-guard. You better be ready to get hit, and you're going to get hit a lot. D-Mac hit me with a flurry of hard lefts. He split my eyebrow right above my nose for 28 stitches. He actually stopped me in the middle of the fight. "Barney, stop!" I kept on going. "I told you to stop," he said, and he grabbed me. "You're leakin' oil bad, Barney." All of a sudden it was like someone turned on a faucet on my forehead and the blood gushed down my face. The game was on national TV, so my family—including my kids—and friends were watching. I got stitched up and called home. My kids were crying. I didn't want my kids to see their dad getting beaten up, with a gash across his face. I see that scar every morning when I look in the mirror.

We played two nights later in Detroit. I had a broken nose and couldn't eat because I had so many cuts in my mouth. I remember being in the corner in that second game, and D-Mac asked, "You don't want to go again, do you?" I replied, "No. No way," and he countered with, "Good! I don't want to go again either." I said, "*You* don't wanna go? I'm here with a face that looks like ground beef!"

There was a fraternity between guys who fight. There was an understanding. We knew what we went through every single day. I don't think any of us loved our roles, but we knew it was the role we had, and we did it willingly, putting our bodies on the line for our teammates and to contribute to our teams. The heavyweights knew their jobs. They're some of the best guys you'll meet, even today. Now that I do events, it's the heavyweights who seem to be the funniest guys.

Tony Granato gave us a blueprint, and we all followed it. We were pretty banged up, though. Teemu Selanne had issues with his knees and Peter Forsberg was really hurt with bad ankles. Nothing against David Aebischer, but I think this team was just a top-flight goalie away from the Cup. Look what happened when they got Patrick Roy. You need a guy who can steal you a few games. But to be there and be part of that team was really special.

Being away from my family was really hard. My kids were still really young, although they came out to visit me once during the playoffs. Even though I had produced on the third line in the regular season, I was put on the fourth line for the playoffs. I was on a line to shut down Mike Modano's line, and we beat Dallas four games to one in the first round of the playoffs but were eliminated by San Jose in the second round.

It was the best six months of my NHL career if you don't consider the 1997–98 season with Buffalo when we went to the semifinals. I loved the role I was given in Colorado. I loved the guys I played with; I loved the coaching staff; I loved the GM, Pierre Lacroix, God rest his soul; and I loved Denver. Even though I was only there for a short period of time, I had a good thing in Colorado, and in hindsight I should have signed there, but my family was on the East Coast. My wife was far away from her parents. I looked for a place to play closer to home.

* * *

You only really get a chance to hit free agency once, and when I became an unrestricted free agent following the 2003–04 season, it was my turn to cash in, plus I wanted to give myself a chance to win the Stanley Cup. Money comes first because you never know how long you are going to be able to play the game. I wanted to set up my family, so I wanted that money in the bank so I didn't have to worry about my kids ever having to struggle like I did.

I had been making $1.5 million a season and thought I'd be able to sign with a team in the $2 million range. Although I had a good offer from Colorado, a four-year term but for less money, I signed a three-year deal with a bit more money with Dale Tallon, the GM of the Chicago Blackhawks. It was also closer to home for my wife and kids. I spoke to other teams, but they wanted me to hold off until the lockout was over because they didn't know what the future held. I made the wrong fucking choice. Hindsight is 20/20, but I should have taken the Colorado deal.

In free agency, you try to find the right situation that will give you what you're looking for. I was looking for success and security. I ended up picking the wrong spot. In hindsight, I wish I had signed with Colorado or waited until after the lockout to see what other opportunities might have presented themselves.

The writing was on the wall that there was going to be a lockout. I treated that summer like every off-season. I took a little bit of time off and then I worked out hard, hoping that there'd be a resolution to the lockout. The NHL lockout resulted in the 2004–05 season being canceled altogether. The main battle was over the league wanting to implement a salary cap, and the National Hockey League Players' Association (NHLPA) was opposed to it.

I had arguments about the salary cap with Bob Goodenow, the NHLPA's executive director. He contended that there was no reason that we shouldn't have a salary cap. One evening, I was sitting around at my house having a few cocktails with Michael Peca and Jay McKee. It was about 11:00 that night, and I called up Goodenow and put him on speaker. I told him, "I'm a big poker player, Bob, and if I am gambling $2 billion of players' money without knowing the outcome, you better have pocket aces and not pocket twos. We are going against billionaires who are going to fall on their swords on this fight. I don't have the education you do, Bob, but I know poker, and I don't see us winning this one."

In September my agent called me and asked if I had any interest in going to Sweden for the 2004–05 season. I told him yes, I wanted to go over and spend the season there. I wanted to stay in game shape. I had my equipment ready and my bags packed, and as I went to leave the house, my son and daughter were crying and each one was hanging on to a leg. They begged me not to go. I looked at my wife and looked at the kids, and I just couldn't do it. I called Larry Kelly, my agent, and told him to call the team in Sweden and tell them that I couldn't go. I couldn't be in Europe with my kids in Buffalo, crying, so I pulled the plug on it.

During the lockout, a bunch of guys in the Buffalo area rented the ice four days a week and we skated and did our normal workouts at the gym. It was very monotonous. It was a grind and was tough to stay motivated.

In January 2005 we thought there was a chance that the season was going to start, but it didn't happen. The lockout wiped out the entire season, and the Stanley Cup wasn't presented for the first time since the Spanish flu wiped out the Final in 1919!

In February 2004 ESPN had named the Blackhawks the worst franchise in professional sports. It was tough playing in Chicago. I'm an emotional player who feeds off the fans, and at that time, we weren't drawing crowds. There'd be 6,000 fans in a 21,000-seat building. We were giving away free tickets just to get spectators into the seats. We weren't on TV in Chicago, either.

The team was rebuilding, so I thought I was going to go there and be a big part of the rebuild. We expected that it was going to take three years to turn the team around, but then the Blackhawks signed a bunch of veterans. They brought in Adrian Aucoin from the Islanders; Curtis Brown, who was my linemate in Buffalo; Jassen Cullimore from Tampa; Nikolai Khabibulin from Edmonton; and Marty Lapointe from Boston. Trent Yawney was our coach. I didn't have much of a role there. I left Colorado, where there was a winning culture, and arrived in Chicago, where the culture was toxic.

I hung out with Marty Lapointe. He was a great leader—a great guy with a work ethic that was off the charts. But Tyler Arnason, Mark Bell, and Kyle Calder really ran the team. I loved going out on the road and having a few drinks, but in my view, if you do, you better come to work and be the hardest worker the next day. It was completely the opposite in Chicago. Those guys partied like rock stars and sometimes didn't even show up for practice the next day. They were our first power-play unit. Don't get me wrong—they were really good guys, but there was a losing culture there. At the end of the season, I sat with Dale Tallon, our general manager, and I told him, "You're not going to have success with this organization with those guys as your leaders."

Again I was cast in the role of enforcer in Chicago, playing on the fourth line and fighting the heavyweights every night. I didn't feel I was used in the most effective way. Despite having a limited role, I still put up 28 points and led the team with 178 penalty minutes in the 2005–06 season.

The team wasn't very good. We finished second-to-last in the NHL. I had hoped to be part of the process to grow the team, but it didn't work out that way. Dale called me into his office and told me that he loved me as a person and as a player, but the team was moving in a different direction and the Hawks were going to buy me out of the final year of my three-year contract. My first year had turned into the lockout season, and I played that 2005–06 with them. I had to respect that, and I appreciated his honesty.

At the 2006 NHL Entry Draft, Chicago selected Jonathan Toews from the University of North Dakota. Interestingly, they also traded Mark Bell to the San Jose Sharks, and Kyle Calder was dealt to the Philadelphia Flyers. The culture changed, as history has recorded.

I found myself as a free agent once again. I didn't have a lot of offers. I signed with the Dallas Stars for 2006–07 and quickly learned that I was the heavyweight again, fighting every single night. Dave Tippett was the coach there, and he was great, and I loved Doug Armstrong, the general manager. I was part of the leadership group, but I knew my career was winding down. I couldn't have played for a better organization. I loved my time in Dallas. The respect I have for Doug Armstrong, the GM, is immense, and Dave Tippett is one of the best coaches I ever played for. Plus, I got to play with Mike Modano, Brenden Morrow, Marty Turco, and Sergei Zubov. Eric Lindros, my friend from the Rangers days, was my roommate again. All the guys were great.

When I arrived, there weren't a lot of vocal guys in the room. Mike Modano and Brenden Morrow were great leaders, but they were quiet and showed their leadership on the ice. I talked to Doug Armstrong and Dave Tippett, and they invited me to step up. As a veteran presence, I made a lot of the dressing room speeches—for season ticket holders, for sponsors. I don't mind talking, and almost immediately, I became one of the faces of the franchise. I was able to speak to the guys, and they listened. At training camp, even though I was new and the guys didn't know me at all, we scheduled a scavenger hunt when we went to Tampa for three days. It was great fun, and at the conclusion, we all met up at the pool. It was one of the first days we all gathered as a group. Entrance to the pool area required bikinis, so here were all these athletes laughing and squeezed into bikinis.

I didn't play much, and when I did, it was to stir things up. I fought more than 400 times in Junior, the AHL, and the NHL. It caught up to me in my last two fights, which I detailed a little bit in chapter 1. On December 20, 2006, I got into that fight with Shawn Thornton in Anaheim when we played the Ducks. Shawn is a tough guy. I played with him in Chicago and tried to convince management to keep him with the big club because it would take some of the pressure off me to fight. We started to throw some punches. I got a couple of licks in, but he pulled my helmet off and landed some punches to my head. We ended up against the end boards, and the linesmen approached us to break up the fight, but we told them to back away. Shawn hit me a few more times and we wrestled until the officials stepped in.

I went to the locker room, put ice on my head, and took a couple of Advils. I was near the end of my career, but I didn't want it to end that way. I couldn't see out of my right eye. The trainer came into the room and asked if I was okay. I said, "Yeah, yeah. Let's go!" When I went back out for the next period, I still couldn't see out of that eye, so I asked my other winger if we could switch sides so I could play on the right side. That way, I could see the ice better.

I never told the team that I couldn't see out of my right eye. If I had, they'd have taken me out of the lineup. I played through it but switched to the other side. Instead of playing left wing, I switched to right wing just so I could see out of that eye. I had headaches for the next few days. A couple of games later, on January 9, 2006, we played Phoenix in Dallas. I fought Josh Gratton. We were right in front of the Coyotes bench. He could really throw them and hit me with a couple, knocking my helmet off. I still couldn't really see out of my right eye, but I tried to hang in there and got a couple of punches in.

I played through the rest of the game and took a couple of Advils. I remember being on the highway home, and I told my wife to pull over. I was puking on the side of the highway. I had a brutal headache when we got home.

I had played a long time and had never had those symptoms. I turned to my wife and told her, "I think it's over. I don't think I can do this anymore." The punches were affecting me, and they weren't even heavy punches. That was two fights in a row. I was seeing double and had spots in my eyes. I told her, "I just can't physically do it anymore."

I went to the rink the next day and told the team I couldn't practice. I had headaches the entire week. I sat down with Dave Tippett and Doug Armstrong and told them that I thought I needed to go back to Buffalo to see Dr. Elad Levy, one of the top neurosurgeons in the United States.

We put together a DVD compilation of my fights, and together we broke down the last two fights, including what I was feeling. He looked me straight in the eyes and said, "Maybe you've never been knocked out, but the punches you have taken through your career have accumulated. If you keep doing this, the symptoms are going to get a lot worse, Matthew. You've had a great career. You're a smart guy. If you want to get to know your kids and coach your son and be there for your daughter and go to her dance recitals, I suggest you quit playing." It was at that moment that I made the decision that that was the end—I had played my final game in the NHL.

I took that back with me to Dallas. I told them my situation but told them I'd like to skate with the team. Normally injured players are kept away from the team. It's almost as though you have the plague, but Doug Armstrong and Dave Tippett made me feel like I was still part of the team. I would skate with the guys every single day. Usually injured players don't travel with the team either, but they included me on the trips. Doug and Dave had me working with the younger players. I bag-skated the guys. I'd be the "rabbit" and they'd chase me.

Dallas finished third in the Pacific Division and made the playoffs. There was no chance I was going to play, but I went with the Stars to Vancouver. I worked out the young guys and the Black Aces after practices during that first round of the playoffs, bag-skating them, but the Canucks eliminated us in seven games.

I really appreciated my time in Dallas. Doug Armstrong and Dave Tippett were such classy guys. Every player wants to be able to end his career on his own terms, and I didn't get that opportunity, but I loved my year in Dallas. It was awesome to finish my playing career surrounded by great people. I ended my career having played 834 regular-season games in the NHL and 62 playoff games—not bad for a guy who got cut from his Midget team!

CHAPTER 10

MOST MEMORABLE GAMES

All-Star Team, 10 years old, 1983.

Nepean Hotspurs, summer 1984.

First hockey team, Hawthorne Hawks, 1979.

Just traded to Verdun, 1993.

AHL 1993–94, Rochester Americans.

My first-ever goal in the NHL.

Celebrating for my favorite fan.

A Mother's Day hat trick.

Saying hi to Caps fans after tying it late in the conference finals.

This is the hardest I was ever hit.

Tie Domi, one of the toughest ever.

I often get asked who the toughest guy I ever fought was, and I always answer, "*Every* guy." *Getty Images / Graig Abel*

"Sabre"-toothed in Buffalo.

Always let 'em see you smile.

I loved my time playing
with the Pens and Jaromir Jagr.
Pittsburgh Penguins Archives

Taunting Isles fans after scoring. What a rivalry! *Getty Images / Bruce Bennett*

I loved playing with Mess.

Mom and bro after a game in the AHL.

Amerks Cruise with Rhonda, summer 1994.

At the ESPYs with Matty Jr.

On the ice with Taylor.

ALMOST EVERY CANADIAN BOY has played the scenario through his head a million times. Outside, playing street hockey, the clock ticking down in overtime—Game 7, of course—three, two, one: "Barnaby scores! Barnaby scores! Barnaby scores! The Montreal Canadiens win the Stanley Cup!"

That was my dream. I never played for Montreal, but they were my childhood favorites. When you finally achieve your dream of making the NHL, you start to realize that everything is a process. You take it one day at a time, but it doesn't take long for you to realize just how damn hard it is to win the Stanley Cup, and how incredibly hard it is just to get there.

I played 834 games over 14 years and never played in a Stanley Cup Final. I made the conference finals once, and we lost to the Washington Capitals in six games in the spring of 1998.

There was only one time when I felt I had a legitimate shot at winning it all. That was 2004, when I was traded to the Colorado Avalanche at the deadline. Unfortunately, we had some injuries, and David Aebischer was simply not a goalie who could get it done for that long a run. I would have loved nothing more than to have a ring and my name on the Cup, but it's not a regret. I did everything in my power to help my teams win the Stanley Cup. I just wasn't fortunate enough, but I did get to play in some really memorable games.

I'll never forget my first-ever game in the National Hockey League at Buffalo Memorial Auditorium—the Aud. I had just signed and was full of piss and vinegar. Old school. I was sporting a mullet. The game is kind of a blur because every shift I went a million miles an hour trying to hit everything in sight, ready to fight anyone and trying to show the fans that I was going to be a force to be reckoned with. I didn't touch the puck a lot, but I did fight Sean Hill. It was a very even fight. What a dream come true! I was in the National Hockey League, doing what I had played out in my mind so many times. It was even cooler than I could have imagined. The guys, the stadium, the fans—wow!

Then there was Montreal in the 1998 playoffs. We were up one game to none in the series. By then I was a solid NHL player, but I was having a terrible year—5 goals and 25 points. But then suddenly I caught fire. It was May 10, 1998. The timing was incredible! My son, Matthew, was born on May 2, and on Mother's Day, with my mom in the stands and my baby boy at home, everything clicked.

On the first goal, I rented Gretzky's office behind the net. I faked one way, went back the other, and stuffed a wraparound through the legs of Andy Moog in the Montreal goal. Obviously, a celebration followed, pointing to a Habs fan in the stands.

In the second period I went in on a two-on-one with my centerman and roomie, Curtis Brown. I faked a pass, dropped one knee, and saw an opening. Half-slapper along the ice. Oh, baby! The score was 5–3, and I had goals four and five in the game.

Later the net was open. I picked up a pass in the neutral zone, skated with it over the blue line, and crossed the defenseman. I went to my backhand and saucered it over the stick of the D-man into the empty net. Hat trick! A natural hat trick!

My mom and family were watching the game from a box. I looked up, spotted them, and saw my mom going insane! (She had probably been served too much wine.) I pointed at her, and the feeling was incredible! I still get shivers thinking about it. What no one remembers is that I also had an assist in that game. Four points in a playoff game against my childhood team, on Mother's Day, with my mom in the stands and a brand-new baby boy at home. It doesn't get any better than that! Nothing can compare to that feeling!

And then: Wayne Gretzky. Do I need to say more? It was April 18, 1999, at Madison Square Garden. Although it was a regular-season game, it was one I'll never forget. It was just another game for us, but there wasn't anyone who didn't have the history in the back of their mind. I don't even remember how much I played, or if I was remotely effective. What I do remember is that it was the Great One's final game in the National Hockey League. He's the greatest player of all time, and a player I grew up watching every Saturday night until 4:00 in the morning on Sunday. It was the only game in my life when I was thinking more about growing up and having a chance to play against Wayne Gretzky and him being an idol when I was a kid. And I was going to have a chance to play in that last game.

I literally sat on the bench looking across to the Rangers bench. And every single shift, he wore different gloves and used a different stick. Knowing it was his final game, he gave a game-used stick to each of his teammates, to special friends, and to the Hockey Hall of Fame. And I was there, a part of history.

I remember tapping him on the pads. Normally I would want to run over him or be the focal point, but not on that day. Not a chance I would try to hit Gretzky in that game. Give me a minus—I don't care. Everyone else was fair game but not No. 99 that night. We ended up winning in overtime with Jaromir Jagr scoring. It was kind of like a passing of the torch the way the game ended.

We all stayed to watch Gretzky take his final turns around the Madison Square Garden ice, saluting the crowd as he went. It was a truly amazing night that I'll never forget, but what has made it even more special is that I have gotten to know Wayne post-career and playing in his golf tournament, playing in his fantasy camp. I can tell you that Wayne Gretzky is the most humble, kind, and first-class superstar you could ever meet.

Just playing in the NHL was memorable, but some games certainly stand out more than others. It was a dream to be able to play in the greatest league in the world.

CHAPTER 11

YOU CAN'T SAY THAT!

IT WAS SATISFYING TO KNOW that I was an NHL player. Even though I had been a good scorer in Junior, I was never going to be a top six forward in the NHL, but I knew what it would take for me to be effective at the NHL level. My role was "shit disturber."

I grew up in an era when anything went. Teachers would walk by, and if you weren't paying attention, you might catch a ruler on your fingers to snap you out of your daydreaming. Coaches would berate you to try to motivate you. Was it right? Hell no! But we didn't know any better. We have gone to the opposite extreme today. You can't say anything to anyone without someone being hurt or ridiculed for it. Maybe it's me, but I think there has to be a middle ground.

After my NHL career ended, I coached at the Junior level. It's the highest and best level before turning pro, with players ranging from age 16 to 20. I saw a player get suspended for two games for calling another player a pussy! Come on! I listened to these players every day, and the shit that came out of their mouths was a thousand times worse than that. Everything now is about perception. Thank God I played when I did, because I wouldn't have played a game now! The shit I said and the shit that was said to me was nasty, but everybody did it—coaches, players, fans. Nothing was sacred.

I was a pest—brash and cocky. I could be vile at times, although I stuck to one personal rule, as I said before: I didn't bring kids or dogs into my chirps, but wives, girlfriends, mothers, and past legal problems were all fair game. And I challenged myself to come up with creative verbal jabs. I yelled from the bench all game long. People always ask me what I said to piss people off, and what follows is a sampling.

Ken Hitchcock was a big man who had battled weight problems through his adult life, but he was fair game for me. He was coaching the Columbus Blue Jackets and was yelling at me from the bench. He had those extra chins that come with being fat, so as I skated past their bench, I grabbed the skin under my neck and made gobbling sounds like a turkey. All of his players were killing themselves laughing! Every time I passed his bench, I'd say, "Hitch, you've got something on your chin! No, the third one!"

Kenny Jonsson was a Swedish defenseman for the New York Islanders, but the poor kid had a terrible problem with his complexion. His face was red from being covered with acne. He skated past our bench, and I screamed, "Kenny, in this country, we eat the pizza. We don't sleep in it!" Our guys howled with laughter.

There was a team that was notorious for using cocaine, and I told their coach, "Thank God you're not on the ice. You would have snorted the red and blue lines!" I shouldn't have been surprised that he sent one of his enforcers out the next time I was on the ice, but he just laughed along with me.

I told Jean-Yves Leroux, "You better sit down or I'll bang your wife… again!" I had dated his wife back when I was in Junior.

Donald Brashear was a fighter, but I'd get under his skin. "The only thing that's tough on you is your breath!" I told him.

Eric Lindros was hyped before he set foot on the ice in a Junior game. He came off as entitled, playing the game on his own terms. He refused to play for the Soo Greyhounds, who drafted him, and ended up being traded so he could play closer to home with the Oshawa Generals.

He later refused to play for the Quebec Nordiques, who drafted him, and ended up being traded to the Philadelphia Flyers. But he was so good he could get away with it. Guys like me sure couldn't. And Eric's parents, Carl and Bonnie, were very active in his career, which I took full advantage of. Every opportunity I had, I'd skate by Eric and ask, "Did Mommy let you play today?" It pissed him off. But we ended up playing together with the Rangers and the Stars and became roommates and good friends.

When tough kids came up from the minors, I'd chirp at them: "I won't even bother learning your name because you'll be back on the buses tomorrow," or "Hey, if you need some extra cash, you can wash my Mercedes after the game!"

I was all over Claude Lemieux during the 1995 playoffs because I knew I could get him off his game. He was easy to agitate, and I knew he was in the midst of a messy divorce, so I went at him with stuff about his wife. Lemieux flipped out and went to Kerry Fraser, the referee, to complain. He tried to get Kerry to stop me from talking about his wife. Kerry called me over and asked if I had said some obscene things about Lemieux's estranged wife, and I admitted, "Yeah, I said those things." Kerry told me to apologize to Lemieux or else he'd kick me out of the game with a gross misconduct. "No way," I said. "You'd never do that." He said, "Oh, yeah? Try me!" I gave Claude a half-hearted apology, and Kerry said, "Not good enough," so I apologized again, and both Fraser and Lemieux thanked me. I may have apologized to save a game misconduct, but I didn't mean a word of it.

If guys were chirping at me, I could usually shut them up pretty quickly with, "You're the cumshot your mom should have swallowed!" If they were yelling at me from the bench, I'd grin and say, "Get your coach's cock out of your mouth so I can understand you!"

I can't take credit for the next two, but it gives you an idea of how guys will say anything to get an edge on an opponent.

Michal Grosek was playing with us in Buffalo. Jim Kyte was a big 6'5" defenseman, and it was well-known that he was deaf. In fact, he was the first legally deaf player to play in the NHL. After Kyte was checked by Rob Ray, Michal went over to Kyte and said, "Hey, Jimmy! Razor hit you so hard that you can probably hear again!" Maybe it's just as well that Kyte didn't hear Grosek, although I know he could read lips!

Another one I witnessed came about in a game we had against the Atlanta Thrashers. The Penguins had offered Billy Tibbetts a professional tryout (PTO) for the 2000–01 season. He had just served 39 months in prison for multiple offenses and had not played hockey in four seasons, but he earned a spot with the Wilkes-Barre Penguins, Pittsburgh's AHL affiliate. After collecting 38 points in 38 games, he got called up to Pittsburgh. Darcy Hordichuk, who was known for his physical play and fighting—he even trained with a mixed martial arts fighter to improve his on-ice fighting—was playing for the Thrashers. Hordichuk started pushing Tibbetts, trying to instigate a fight, but Tibbetts just looked at him and said, "You think I'm afraid of you? I fucked a lot bigger guys than you in the ass when I was in prison."

Now you understand why guys wanted to kill me. That's what I wanted! I wanted them to come after me and punch me or slash me so that we could win the game. That's what it was all about—winning! Bruises hurt a lot less when you win. That was my job, and I loved being public enemy number one! I wanted every fan base to despise me and every franchise that I played for to love me.

I was going to fake an injury. I was going to dive. I didn't care! I was going to do whatever it took to win! During the playoffs in 1998, I faked a high stick in overtime, and with our power play, we scored and won the game, and with that we clinched the series. The stick came close to me but didn't get me. I had to sell it to make sure the referees felt certain it was a penalty.

The year before, I took a stick to the face. I immediately pulled my silver teeth out of my mouth and showed Kerry Fraser that my teeth had been knocked out with the high stick. He called a five-minute major on the player. The same thing happened a couple games later, but this time, Kerry said, "You little bastard! You're not getting me again!" I forgot that he was the official I had pulled the stunt on the first time!

I took it as my job to get under the skin of opponents. If I could goad players to retaliate against my verbal jabs by taking a penalty against me, then guys such as Patty LaFontaine could hop over the boards on the power play and score a goal for us. If the player took a swing at me, I wasn't afraid to go, and in Buffalo, we had Rob Ray and Brad May to take on anyone else who took exception to my chirps. There was a reason I was hated by opponents but loved by my teammates and the fans.

CHAPTER 12

THE FIGHT CLUB

I NEVER GREW UP WANTING TO FIGHT, especially against men who were way bigger than me. That would have been just plain stupid! I knew I had to fight if I was going to play in the National Hockey League and, more important, if I were going to have a long career playing the game I loved at the highest level.

It was a breath of fresh air when I dropped the gloves against someone about my size—six feet tall and 190 pounds. That was roughly the height and weight I played at for 14 NHL seasons. Don't get me wrong—there were some really tough guys at that size, but the punches felt different. That is probably why boxing and UFC have competitors in certain weight classes. Mike Tyson wasn't going to fight Roy Jones Jr. The difference in power is astronomical. Roy Jones Jr. would be able to dance for a while, but one good punch from Tyson and it would be "Good night."

That wasn't the way it was in the NHL, especially back in the 1990s. Also, there is no dancing around a ring in hockey; you lock in and throw. Trying to avoid the opponent's "big one" is a must, as is being calculated enough not to open yourself up to the KO shot. I watched many a guy try to go toe to toe, and in most cases they didn't last long. Guys punched too hard, and the brain can only take so much.

Almost everywhere I go, I get asked who the toughest guy I fought was, but I answer the question the same way every time. *Every* guy is the toughest, because at any moment, they can send you to sleep, or to the hospital with a broken face. You can never, ever be overconfident or cocky in a fight, because if you are, it won't end well. Are there guys who made me more nervous to fight? Yes, absolutely! But everyone who played that role was in it for a reason, just like I was.

Just like you study tape on an opposing team's power play and penalty kill, you study fights too. I needed to know how the guys fought. Were they lefties or righties? Did they try for the knockout punch right away? Did they try to go under an arm so you couldn't hang on? So many things go into being an effective fighter, and you have to be prepared.

I knew I didn't stand a chance at winning fights with some of the guys I fought, but if our team was sluggish or not playing well, I would try to change the momentum of the game by dropping my gloves against one of the opposing team members. Zdeno Chara was one of those guys. We fought three or four times. Was I insane? The fucking guy is 6'9" and 265 pounds. That sure wasn't my weight class!

I watch some of the fights with Chara now, and I didn't get killed, didn't get cut, and didn't get thrown around like a rag doll. I approached the fights knowing that I wanted to rotate and spin and try to jump up to hit him, but in doing so, I didn't give up the "kill shot." I couldn't stand toe to toe with a guy such as Chara because my arms simply wouldn't reach. In a fight with Chara, a draw was a win, plus it pumped up the team and the fans. These kinds of fights drag your team into battle on nights they might not have it.

Stu Grimson was another one—6'5" and 250 pounds. You don't get the nickname "the Grim Reaper" because you're a power-play specialist! You get it because you are mean and nasty, and 9 times out of 10, you inflict a lot of pain on the other guy.

One night in Pittsburgh, I was out against Stu and the puck went into the corner. The whistle was blown, and Grimson and I just glared at each other. His fear level of me was a solid 0 out of 10, but I asked him to go. He waited for me to drop my gloves so he didn't get sucked into a penalty. I dropped my gloves and hit him. He didn't budge. The referees came in. The faceoff was outside the zone, and I was lined up beside him. Stu asked, "Are you ready to go?" Just as he asked, Jaromir Jagr tapped me and called me for a change of lines. I shook him off and told Jags, "No fucking way!" I had to go with Grimson. Jagr returned to the bench, knowing full well that my pride and 16,000 fans were waiting for us to go. As soon as the puck dropped, I was backing up, trying to figure out how to attack him. We locked in and I glanced up. He was fucking large! And so strong. He started to punch, not even concerned about what might be coming his way. I shielded my face and took punches but refused to go down. He continued to pummel me as he said, "Go down!" I refused. He looked over at the refs and they stepped in, stopping the fight. We went to the penalty box. I got a loud ovation from the Pittsburgh faithful. I lost—by a lot—but I showed up. I had no chance of winning, but I survived.

Fighting is part of the game of hockey and always will be, but I do like the fact that it isn't the way now that it was. Too many people have been hurt really badly. I'm sure that one day I will find out about fighting's long-term effects, but I would never change the way I played. I knew that at any point, I could get hurt—maybe even badly enough to end my career. I chose to play the way I did because I wanted to play in the best league in the world, and playing that way was my key to the NHL. I loved the respect I got in the dressing room from everyone, including the coaches and the trainers, but especially from the guys I played with who knew I had their backs and would do anything for the team, even if it risked my safety.

The most popular guys on the team are the scorers, the goalies, and the tough guys. Some players will tell you that it's not a big deal, but when fans are chanting your name or when you see people wearing jerseys with your name and number, it's a rush, and we all have an ego.

Part of me wishes I could play in today's era, but *wow*, did I ever love the era I played in! It might sound a little off, but remember, it wasn't Matthew Barnaby fighting—it was somebody else wearing the No. 36 jersey who was definitely a little off!

CHAPTER 13

THE SMILE, BABY

WHEN I DECIDED TO TAKE ON THE ROLE of a "rat," I quickly realized that it is more mental than physical. I always played hard, trying to ride the line without going over it. It's a challenge, because you need to be a pain in the ass to opponents without putting your team at a disadvantage. Being at a disadvantage doesn't help your team at all and is not effective. Mentally you know that the other team is going to try to get you off your game or say shit to piss you off so you'll take a penalty. Many tried with me, but it just didn't work. It's what I did during the game, so I wasn't letting anyone live rent-free in my head. No fucking way!

We have all argued with someone, and when you do and continue to try to prove your point, it proves that it bothers you. If anyone has ever smirked at you or laughed at you during an argument, you know how it pisses you off beyond words. That's why I smiled when I was challenging guys on the other team. It made them crazy! I knew I could say the nastiest shit or whack a guy behind the legs, because at some point, the guy's emotions would take over.

There were times when I fought guys who were much bigger than me and much tougher than me, and I knew I was not going to win the fight. But I was not going to lose the mental side. That's why I smiled. Why would I smile in the middle of fights? It was because it got the other guy so fucking mad! He'd lose his mind, and at that point, he might change the way he fought me or think that I was done, and then I could surprise him. People don't think straight when they are in a rage.

It was all calculated by me. I loved to watch a guy punch and punch and punch and not be able to beat me. I might have lost the fight, but I was going to smile and laugh so that when we got out of the box, he might lose his mind and come at me again. That time I would know he wanted to kill me, but depending on the score, I had him set up to take a penalty. I would ask him to fight and watch him drop his gloves and start whaling on me. Then I would put my head down, gloves still on, and take some punches—not because I was afraid but because winning was more important. He would draw a two-minute roughing minor or maybe even a five-minute major, and we would have a power play, baby! I would then look him square in the eyes and tell him how stupid he was. Big smile! And if we scored with the extra man, my smile would be as big as that of a fat kid with chocolate cake!

I can go back in my career and think of all the penalties I drew from opponents. Part of it was playing really hard and part of it was things I said, but the number one reason was because I infuriated guys on the other team with the smile. That's why it was a no-brainer for me to have silver teeth with the Sabres logo put in my mouth. "Come and get it, boys! Rip it right out of my fucking mouth!" It put us on the power play many times.

One of my favorite lines came from Darren Pang, a former NHL goaltender who became an excellent broadcaster. TSN did a list of the all-time greatest agitators, and I was voted No. 1. Panger said, "If I was a player on another team, I would want to sucker punch Matthew Barnaby."

CHAPTER 14

SUPERSTAR TEAMMATES

I GREW UP—like many young boys—idolizing the best players in the NHL. My favorite player was Mats Naslund, not only because he was good but also because he was a Montreal Canadien, my favorite team. I also loved watching Steve Yzerman, Wayne Gretzky, Mario Lemieux, and many others, hoping one day I'd play in the NHL just like them. Once you get to the Show, at first you just try to survive, and then you want to become a regular. Although I never allowed myself to get starstruck, it seemed that every game I played, I was facing one of the players I grew up watching.

Pat LaFontaine

It started in Buffalo, where I had the opportunity to play with Pat LaFontaine. Patty was our captain, and he very well might be the nicest person I've ever met. He'd remember your grandmother's name after meeting her once two years before. His skill was ridiculous, his skating was so smooth, but what people don't realize is just how funny he is. Patty loved to play poker too. He was an amazing teammate. Injuries really plagued him in Buffalo, but when he was healthy, he was dominant. He led the team in scoring in 1992–93, when I played my first NHL games, and again in 1995–96. The Sabres traded him to the New York Rangers before the 1997–98 season, and tragically he suffered a career-ending head injury against Ottawa in March 1998. A sad end to a phenomenal career. We all loved Patty.

ALEXANDER MOGILNY

Alex Mogilny was already several years into his NHL career by the time I joined the Sabres. He was an elite goal scorer—in 1992–93 he scored 76 goals! Alex had unreal chemistry with Patty LaFontaine. When Patty was injured in 1993–94, Almo—his nickname—filled in as our captain. He was a fun guy but pretty much kept to himself. He was traded to the Vancouver Canucks in the off-season after the 1994–95 season. Of all the superstars I played with, he's the only one who isn't in the Hockey Hall of Fame. It's a big omission—this guy belongs in there!

GRANT FUHR

Grant Fuhr was likely the quirkiest Hall of Famer I ever played with. He came to the Sabres in a trade with Toronto in February 1993, and later that season, I played my first NHL games. Grant was older and had already won the Stanley Cup five times with Edmonton. Imagine this: In my first three years in Buffalo, we had Dominik Hasek and Grant Fuhr as our goalies—two of the greatest goalies ever! In fact, in 1993–94 they shared the Jennings Trophy for the lowest team goals-against average. Grant was always in a good mood, laughing and telling stories. He didn't stress about anything! The Sabres traded him to L.A. in February 1995.

JAROMIR JAGR

In Pittsburgh I was fortunate to play with both Mario Lemieux and Jaromir Jagr. Jagr was a goofball, but man, he strove to be the best every day. His combination of unreal hands and a wicked wrist shot was lethal to opponents. And he was 6'4" and 245 pounds! He was the Penguins' captain while I was in Pittsburgh, and he led the NHL in scoring in the three seasons I played there. In 1998–99 he had 127 points, in 1999–2000 he had 96, and in 2000–01 he had 121 points. He was dominant. I was traded to Tampa in February 2001, and Jags was traded to Washington later that summer.

MARIO LEMIEUX

Mario is the epitome of class and carries himself that way. I don't know if a player ever made the game look easier. He was very reserved but did like to joke around at times.

He hadn't played for three seasons, and I think everybody thought he was done. We would see him around the rink, but in December 2000 we heard he might try to make a comeback. Unbelievable! He stepped back onto the ice like he'd never been gone, and in 43 games he had 76 points!

MARTIN ST. LOUIS

Tampa Bay was a low point for me, but it was pretty cool to play with the hardest-working Hall of Famer, Marty St. Louis. Marty had the skill of a really good player, but it was his work ethic that got him into the Hockey Hall of Fame. Marty was an unreal teammate. Tampa's best players were young guys: Vinnie Lecavalier, Brad Richards, and Marty. I was gone by then, but they led Tampa to the club's first Stanley Cup championship in 2004, and Marty won the Art Ross Trophy that year for leading the league in scoring.

MARK MESSIER

I have the ultimate respect for Mark Messier. He was an amazing player. In fact, he would probably be the player I would have loved to have been. Mess had good skill, was a straightforward player, and had incredible hockey sense, but he also had a nastiness that you generally just don't see from Hall of Fame players. His leadership skills were second to none, and his commitment to greatness was unparalleled. He had led the Rangers to the Stanley Cup in 1994, and then in 1997 he joined Mike Keenan in Vancouver. After three seasons there, he returned to the Rangers in 2001–02, the year I was traded to New York. When Mess was in Vancouver, Brian Leetch had been the Rangers' captain, but he handed it back to Mess when he returned. The 2003–04 season was my last in New York because I was traded to Colorado at the trade deadline. That season was Mark Messier's final season. He retired in 2004.

ERIC LINDROS

Eric Lindros and I battled for many years. I'm sure he hated me more than I hated him. But then when I got to New York, we became roommates and good friends. Heck, we even went to Ireland to golf with our buddies one summer—that was something I never could have imagined. If I were going to build a hockey player from scratch, it would be the Big E. He could score, punish your defense physically, and kick the shit out of your tough guy. He would have dominated in any and every era. In 2001–02, my first season with the Rangers, Eric led the team in scoring. Injuries started to take their toll on him, and he missed a lot of the 2003–04 season. That was his final year in New York. He signed as a free agent with Toronto after that.

PAVEL BURE

It might have been near the end of his career, but man, Pavel Bure could score! He was a one-dimensional player with a knack for scoring. Pavel was a fun-loving guy who would disappear once our practice or game was done. You wouldn't see him! He was lightning-quick on the ice and always a threat. The 2002–03 season was his last in the NHL, and even though he missed half the season with a knee injury, he still scored 19 goals in 39 games.

BRIAN LEETCH

Brian Leetch is the most underrated, humble, unassuming Hall of Famer I have ever met. Don't get me wrong—he was very confident and knew he was great, but he would never, ever not treat everyone like an equal. Brian would always wait for wingers to look away, and then he'd jump into holes. He was an unbelievable skater and had a level of competitiveness that was off the charts. Brian had already won two Norris Trophies by the time I arrived in New York, but he was still dominant. Brian went to Toronto at the trade deadline on March 3, 2004, and I was traded to Colorado later that same week.

JOE SAKIC

Joe Sakic was a tremendous leader for the Avalanche. He was quiet but really funny, yet he always knew when his voice needed to be heard. Joe had the quickest wrist shot I ever saw and made the players around him so much better. When I was playing Junior in Quebec, Joe was with the Nordiques, and I used to call him TQS—which was a French TV station. The Quebec Nordiques had some bad teams in their day, but wow, Joe was always great. He'd be chosen as the First Star with three goals and two assists but finish the game a minus-five. I was only in Colorado one season, and Joe led the team in scoring that year.

PAUL KARIYA

Paul Kariya was very quirky, and if he hadn't played hockey, he would not have hung out with athletes, but holy fuck, could he play hockey! He was quick and could turn on a dime, and then there was that wrist shot! Wow! And compete, compete, compete. By far, he did the most pregame presentation and had the greatest focus, but on top of that, he had so many superstitions. I still can't get the sight of Paul getting pinned down by Adam Foote out of my head. It was hilarious to hear the cries and squealing that came out of Paul's mouth.

The 2003–04 season was my only season with the Avalanche, and it was Paul's only season in Colorado too. He missed a lot of that season with a wrist injury.

Teemu Selanne and Paul Kariya were really different guys, but they were the best of friends. They had such great chemistry together. When they played in Anaheim, you just waited for the inevitable when that power play stepped onto the ice: "Goal scored by Teemu Selanne, assisted by Paul Kariya." There was some justice that they were inducted into the Hockey Hall of Fame in the same year, 2017.

TEEMU SELANNE

Teemu was my roommate in Colorado, and he was an unbelievable guy. He was dealing with injuries that year, so it wasn't the Selanne of old. As a rookie with Winnipeg in 1992–93, he had 76 goals! And he led the NHL in goals in 1997–98 and 1998–99 when he was with the Mighty Ducks. Teemu was a great skater. He always got the puck in stride, and then you couldn't catch him. What a tremendous human being!

PETER FORSBERG

Peter Forsberg had it all. He was highly skilled and just a phenomenal passer. Peter would dominate defensemen down low, spinning them until he lost them, they fell, or they were just too fatigued to stay with him. He created the offensive reverse hit, and no matter how ready you were, he always came out with the puck, which usually ended with a faceoff at center ice. That season I played in Colorado, I didn't see Forsberg at his best because he was out with a hip injury for much of the season, but boy, could he play!

ROB BLAKE

Rob Blake had a very similar personality to Brian Leetch off the ice—he was quiet and humble. But on the ice, he was a very different person.

He was physically dominant, had the ability to jump into the rush, and had a really big shot. And he was sneaky. Fuck, if your head was down, nighty-night! He had an ass for days, and he used it to destroy opponents. Rob was a really smart guy too, and I can't say I'm surprised that he is now an executive with the Los Angeles Kings.

*   *   *

Anybody who plays in the National Hockey League is a great player and finds their role on the team. No wonder the NHL is the greatest league in the world. But there are some guys who just rise to the top as superstars, and I was honored to play with so many.

CHAPTER 15

BOYS WILL BE BOYS

IT DOESN'T MATTER HOW OLD men are or the nature of their profession—boys will be boys, and that certainly is true of NHL players. Most players who make it to the Show have sacrificed a great deal since they were very young in order to make it, which includes training when others are partying. Most guys in their early twenties are at frat parties, not preparing to play an NHL game. In many ways, we gave up our childhood years.

One of the best things when you finally make the NHL is rookie initiation. It's not like Junior or the American Hockey League. When I was in Junior, a lot of the hazing that took place was disgusting (as detailed in chapter 6). The AHL was much better. My initiation was in 1994, and drinking was at the core of that initiation. They got us super drunk. Thanks go to my roommate in Rochester, Doug MacDonald, who saved my life, as I was passed out on my back in bed with puke in my mouth. Oh yeah, they shaved our heads too. They left me with a shaved head but left the bangs—now *that's* a hot look!

I never saw any of that in the NHL. The NHL was about inclusion, not demeaning players. Once you've received a couple paychecks, rookies split the bill for an expensive team dinner. And they don't pick the Cracker Barrel. It's the best five-star restaurant in whatever road city the veterans pick. It's a feast that includes $500 bottles of wine!

The tabs range anywhere from $2,500 to $8,000 apiece, depending on how many rookies are present. There have been a few memorable rookie dinners through the years. One was at the Forge in Miami Beach, where strippers danced for guys in a private room. One of the rookies showed up with a stripper as his date at the rookie dinner we had at La Queue de Cheval Steakhouse in Montreal. That was a first, and it was awesome. The most expensive rookie dinner I witnessed was at Ruth's Chris Steak House in Scottsdale, Arizona. I was in charge that year. We all took limos and played golf at the Grayhawk Golf Club, then had dinner. The rookies split a bill that totaled $56,000 American. Not only did I have a great day paid for by somebody else, but I got a hole in one that day! Lots of reasons to celebrate.

* * *

The escapades continued through my career. One night, when I was with the Penguins, we were on Long Island playing the Islanders and we had a huge lead going into the third period. It seems our backup goalie had made a deal with a girl in the first row. I never saw her, but I'm imagining a big-busted blonde. Let's go with that. The deal was that if we scored another goal, he would have security bring the young lady down the back way to the dressing room for some fun. Enter Jaromir Jagr. Jags opened the third with a quick goal, and the girl, as agreed upon, was escorted into the dressing room. Our backup disappeared into the tunnel and into our room. With his equipment still on but loosened, the girl proceeded to drop to her knees and go down on him. They finished rather quickly and returned to the game, her to her seat and our backup to the end of the bench. No one had a clue what had happened until we got on the bus after the game. In my wildest dreams, I never could have imagined that this could happen in the NHL, but it did. The best thing is that the Islanders found out and wanted to report it, but that was quickly squashed. Thank God!

*   *   *

Randy Burridge was a beauty—one of my favorites. He was always happy. He simply loved life. Every summer Randy hosted a golf tournament in Fort Erie, Ontario, which was just across the border from Buffalo. All of the Sabres who lived close by attended each year. On this occasion, I left our home at 7:00 AM and told my wife I'd be home by 11:00 that night. Guys will say anything to get out of the house.

What a day we had: golf, booze, girls, and best buds. I remember looking at my phone at around 10:00 PM, and my wife had left me a message: "Hope you're having fun! See you soon!" I called back and left a message saying, "Absolutely! Leaving soon." I had zero intention of leaving, but my message gave me some room to figure out a plan.

One drink led to 12, and before I realized it, it was 4:00 AM! There were lots of missed calls on my phone—likely 50! I've always adhered to a policy of begging for forgiveness rather than asking for permission.

At 4:30 a bunch of us were crossing the border into the U.S. The agent looked in the window of the limo and said, "Hey, boys. How are we doing tonight?" All cockeyed, we joked with the agent for a few minutes and then I got the bright idea to ask him if he'd call my wife and tell her that I didn't have my P-1 visa, which allows individuals such as athletes who compete at an internationally recognized level to cross the border. The agent said, "Sure, I'll call her."

He picked up the phone, and I heard him say, "Hello. Mrs. Barnaby?" Christine said, "Yes?" and we could hear the worry in her voice. The agent continued, "Don't worry. We have Matthew here. He's been here since 11:30. We had to detain him because he didn't have his P-1 visa to enter the United States. He tried to call you but there was no answer. I just want you to know that he's fine and we are letting him through now."

I promised the agent that I'd leave him two tickets for a Sabres game. It was the best two tickets I ever left for someone.

* * *

We rolled into Chicago about midnight and checked into the Drake Hotel, where we regularly stayed when we played the Blackhawks. We were told that curfew was right away because we had lost. We thought that was ridiculous, so Brad "Mayday" May and I decided we were going to go for a few beers anyway. The only problem was that we couldn't go through the lobby because that was where the coaches always drank.

We called down to the concierge and asked him to come up to our room because we had an issue. When the guy arrived, we told him our predicament and gave him 20 bucks to get us out a different way. The concierge agreed, and we ended up taking stairs and then going through the kitchen's side rooms.

Anyone who knows Mayday knows how pumped and squealy his voice gets when he's excited. "Oh, baby, we did it!" he said. Just as Brad said that, we walked through a door and went into immediate shock! The door led to a bar called the Coq D'Or, and there was John Muckler sitting there! He looked at us and barked, "What the fuck are you guys doing? We have curfew!"

We hemmed and hawed and stammered, "Looking for food. Room service is closed." Jim Kelley, the sports reporter for the *Buffalo News*, chimed in, "Don't think so, boys! There's 24-hour room service."

My heart sank. I was dripping sweat. In that deep, crackly voice of his, Muckler said, "Get the fuck to your rooms!"

This time we took the scenic route back. Nice try, but no cigar.

* * *

Everybody called Rob Ray "Razor." He's a great guy, but man, could I get under his skin! I loved to tease him and have fun with him. One time we were on the bus heading to Buffalo State, where we used to practice. The original one-piece composite sticks had just come out. They were called Busch, and were made by a Swiss company. We all had them, but Razor got his later, and he only got one. It had RAZOR printed on the shaft. It looked great, and he was so proud of it. Rob had it taped up, ready to dump pucks into the corner.

The bus took off, and I asked Razor if I could see his stick. He handed it to me, and I stood up and started leaning on it, checking out the flex. "I love it, man," I said. He replied, "Be fucking careful! I only have one!" I said, "Yeah, yeah. Of course!" Then I looked at him and stepped on the blade. Snap! I broke his stick!

In all my years of knowing him, I had never seen him snap like he did! He started throwing haymakers at me, and I did the same. Brad May and our other teammates were in disbelief as they watched us go at it in full equipment; a full-on brawl on the bus!

We were getting tired and Rob was getting the better of me, but I couldn't stop laughing. That brought out even more rage in Razor. I had his arms tied up so he couldn't punch me. Furious, he was grinding his teeth and then head-butted me in the face! It knocked my bridge out and cut my mouth! I deserved every bit of it! All I remember afterward was Mayday shouting, "Let's get it on! Let's have ourselves a practice!"

CHAPTER 16

THE COACHES' CORNER

SO MUCH IN LIFE is having someone believe in you. You can have the greatest product idea in the world, but with no money, it won't get off the ground. You need investors. If no one believes in your product, it will fail. It's the same in sports. If no one believes in you, your chances of success are slim to none.

When I was in Junior, I was fortunate to have a coach who believed in me. That followed me to the Buffalo Sabres, where I went from a rookie trying to fit in to a regular and then became a core piece. But that can all change in a heartbeat. Coaches and general managers must believe in you or you could be in trouble. There are too many really good players out there just waiting for their shot.

My life has always been what I call PPW—Prove People Wrong. I've had great coaches and great guys and I've had shitty coaches and shitty guys. They don't always align.

JOHN MUCKLER

John Muckler had been a longtime minor league player who moved into coaching after his playing career. He had been an assistant coach with the Edmonton Oilers and served as a co-coach with Glen Sather when they won the Stanley Cup in 1987 and 1988. He was the team's head coach when they won the Cup again in 1990. During the 1991–92 season,

Mucks was hired to coach the Buffalo Sabres. When I played my first games in the NHL in 1992–93, John Muckler was the coach, with John Tortorella and Don Lever as the assistants. John added general manager to his role in 1993–94.

Mucks was an intimidating man—very stern and tough. He showed no compassion but was brutally honest and expected you to play your role. He did cater to the stars but appreciated every member of the team. He challenged us daily! He was a great man and a very smart hockey man. We lost John Muckler on January 4, 2021. Rest in peace, Mucks.

TED NOLAN

Muckler wanted to concentrate on the general manager's role with the Sabres and hired Ted Nolan to coach the team starting with the 1995–96 season. Teddy had been an assistant coach with the Hartford Whalers the year before, but it was his phenomenal success with the Soo Greyhounds of the Ontario Hockey League that really stood out on his résumé.

Teddy Nolan was the perfect coach for me. He had been a player, so he knew a player's sensibilities, but he had also been a coach who knew how to work with his players to find success. X's and O's were not his forte. He was able to delegate to his assistants, Don Lever and Terry Martin in 1995–96 and Lever and Paul Theriault in 1996–97, really well. Teddy coached on emotion. He demanded hard work and competitive spirit over skill. Ted Nolan is a tremendous person, and players would run through a wall for him. He got a second shot with Buffalo when Patty LaFontaine was brought in as president of hockey operations in November 2013. It is a travesty that Ted has not had another shot at being a head coach in the NHL since that time.

LINDY RUFF

I was intensely loyal to Ted Nolan, and after the team had had such success and Teddy was named Coach of the Year, the Sabres only offered him a one-year contract, which he rightly declined. It was apparent to most of us on the team that Muckler wanted Teddy gone, and when he said no to the contract, Mucks hired Lindy Ruff in his place.

Ted Nolan is a great man as well as a great coach, so I was pissed off. I can admit now that I never really gave Lindy a chance, but starting with the 1997–98 season, we had to work together.

Lindy had played in the league for a number of years, and most were with Buffalo. He had been an assistant coach with the Florida Panthers, but when he was hired by Muckler, it was Lindy's first head coaching job.

Lindy was very methodical. He was a smart hockey guy but was very arrogant when he started coaching. We clashed. Our personalities were different, but I also held him responsible for replacing Ted Nolan. I wish I had played for him at a different time.

KEVIN CONSTANTINE

Sometimes you are the smartest person in the room but an asshole. That was Kevin Constantine. He was the coach in Pittsburgh when I was traded there in March 1999.

Constantine had been a goalie in U.S. college hockey. He had coached the San Jose Sharks before he was hired by Pittsburgh. Kevin was a great X's and O's guy but had zero people skills. Zero! He would go so far to prove his point that he lost his core. There was no middle ground—it was his way or die. That's not a recipe with a guy such as Jaromir Jagr. And Constantine didn't like my game. He hated me, and I hated him. I lasted longer in the NHL than he did. I win!

HERB BROOKS

When the Penguins fired Constantine in 1999, he was replaced by Herb Brooks. Herbie had been a longtime U.S. college coach who was behind the bench for the Do You Believe in Miracles? Olympic gold medal–winning Team USA at the Winter Olympics in 1980. He was hired to coach in the NHL with the New York Rangers, Minnesota North Stars, and New Jersey Devils before he was hired in Pittsburgh.

Herbie was like a father as a coach, always trying to teach you lessons. He would call me before games and ask what systems we should play, but he was really just picking my brain. Herb kept us on our toes. He expected *team* before *player*. We were only together for a short time, but it was a great time. Herb Brooks died in a car accident in August 2003. Rest in peace, Herb.

IVAN HLINKA

Ivan Hlinka was born in former Czechoslovakia and played for his country in a number of international tournaments. He was one of the first players who had permission from the country to join the NHL, and he played two seasons with the Vancouver Canucks in the early 1980s.

The Penguins had a crazy number of guys from the Czech Republic on the team in 2000–01: Josef Beranek, Jan Hrdina, Jaromir Jagr, Frantisek Kucera, Robert Lang, Josef Melichar, Michal Rozsival, Roman Simicek, Jiri Slegr and Martin Straka. They were all really good players and really good guys. The Penguins hired a guy from their country who could speak their language—Hlinka. He was the first European-trained head coach in the history of the NHL.

It's crazy to think we were playing in the NHL for a coach who didn't speak English. Ivan Hlinka seemed like a fun-loving, smart hockey guy, but I would have learned more from a Japanese hooker than from what Ivan taught me. He used to constantly borrow my clubs so he could golf with the Czechs on our team in Pittsburgh because we were both lefties. Ivan Hlinka died in a car accident in August 2004. Rest in peace, Ivan.

JOHN TORTORELLA

John Tortorella and I first crossed paths when he was an assistant coach in Buffalo, but I didn't really know him. I got to know him really quickly when I was traded to Tampa Bay in February 2001. He was the head coach there after years as an assistant coach with a bunch of different NHL teams.

Torts has one way—*his*! He wanted us to play with commitment to defense, and no one could stray! He was an asshole at the rink but a kind and compassionate man away from it. Torts thought I stunk as a player but didn't have the support to help me. I definitely respect John Tortorella, but I didn't like playing for him.

RON LOW

I had to get out of Tampa. Torts was honest and told me I didn't fit into his plans. I respected his honesty, but that didn't help my career at all. In December 2001 the Lightning traded me to the New York Rangers, and Ron Low was the coach that season.

Ron Low was an old-school coach. He really let the stars run the team, but we had so many of them that there was zero accountability. Ron was a guy you would love to sit and have a beer with, but he was not a coach to lead you to the Promised Land. He played me a lot, so that was very welcomed, and he resurrected my career, so that was very appreciated.

BRYAN TROTTIER

After the 2001–02 season, Ron Low was fired and Glen Sather, our GM, hired Bryan Trottier. Trots had been a star with the rival Islanders and was on those four consecutive Stanley Cup–winning teams. He had been an assistant coach with Pittsburgh and Colorado, but the Rangers were his first time as a head coach.

Bryan is one of the nicest men I have ever met in hockey, and he was one of the best two-way players ever to play the game, but he was not one of the best coaches I ever played for. His heart was always in the right spot. I consider him a perfect assistant, but Trots was too nice to be a head coach. He got fired partway through that 2002–03 season, and Glen Sather took over behind our bench.

GLEN SATHER

Slats was a hardworking NHL forward, but he really built his reputation as the coach and general manager of the Oilers during the 1980s. Before the 2000–01 season, Glen was hired as the president and general manager of the Rangers.

After he fired Bryan Trottier later in the 2002–03 season, Sather took over as head coach on top of his president and GM roles. I owe a lot to Glen Sather. He traded for me in New York and it revived my career, but he was behind the times as a coach when he took over. His main focus was to keep Jim Dolan, the chairman of Madison Square Garden who owned the team, happy. Slats wanted us to wear the long gloves that Gretzky wore in the 1980s, and he hated that we used composite sticks. He'd yell, "Wood sticks!"

One of my favorite lines that was directed at Glen but said to me on the bench during a practice came from Bobby Holik. "Barney, did they not watch me play for the last 10 years? If I'm on the penalty kill and third-line center, we have a good chance of winning the Cup, but if I'm on the power play and first-line center, we aren't making the playoffs!" Guess what? We didn't make the playoffs.

Glen is a good guy and treated me really well, but he assembled an all-star team, and that doesn't win in the NHL. There just isn't enough ice time to go around for a team of stars.

TOM RENNEY

We started the 2003–04 season with Glen Sather behind the bench, but he later brought in Tom Renney, our assistant coach, to take over as interim head coach. Tom had head coaching experience at the Junior level as well as with Team Canada at various tournaments, including a silver medal at the Olympics in 1994. He also had coached the Vancouver Canucks.

Tom is a very smart man and an even better person. He is very respectful and really knows the game. If Tom had been our coach for the entire season, we would have been a playoff team. Sadly the Rangers missed the playoffs for the seventh straight season.

Tom has great respect in the hockey world, and his knowledge of the game served him well in his later position as president and CEO of Hockey Canada.

TONY GRANATO

Tony Granato was a really good NHL player—hardworking and honest through 13 seasons as a player. He moved into coaching after retiring as a player, and when I was traded to Colorado in March 2004, Tony was in his second season behind the Avalanche's bench.

Tony was great, a real player's coach, but we had a really skilled, veteran team, so he essentially let the room run itself. Tony was tough when he needed to be but defined everyone's roles very well, which was so important. I had 9 points in 13 games when I was traded to Colorado but then was moved to the fourth line in a shutdown role during the playoffs. Tony was a great coach with a great team, but we needed a great goalie to win, which we didn't have.

TRENT YAWNEY

Trent Yawney was an NHL veteran as a player and had been with the Blackhawks as a player twice, totaling six seasons.

As a player there is a big difference between Junior and college and the pros, and a big difference between the AHL and the NHL. Older guys want respect—work us hard but don't treat us like children. Trent was in his first year as a head coach when I played with Chicago in 2005–06. He was a really good guy, but he treated us like kids. He never gained the respect of his players. I think Trent Yawney would have been a way better assistant coach.

DAVE TIPPETT

After a long NHL playing career, Dave Tippett had been a winning coach in the IHL and an assistant coach with the L.A. Kings. When he was hired as the head coach of the Dallas Stars in 2002–03, it was his first time as an NHL head coach, and he was quite successful from the start.

I didn't land in Dallas until 2006–07, and Dave was there then. He was one of my favorite coaches. He was stern but fun, and although he was very much an X's and O's guy, he understood that the game isn't black-and-white, that there are, in fact, some gray areas. Dave treated me really well and understood my role as well as my personality. He was very honest and up-front, which I loved.

* * *

I had a wide variety of coaches through my NHL career. Some were tactical guys and others were players' coaches. Some understood me and others had no clue. Some knew how to best use me and others didn't. Some were great guys and, well…there were also some others. But I appreciate them all to varying degrees for being part of my hockey journey.

CHAPTER 17

LIFE AFTER HOCKEY

WHEN I RETIRED IN 2007, I had played 834 regular-season games. I take great pride in that, especially when I reflect back on getting cut from my teams when I was a teenager. You want to play as long as you are able to and leave on your own terms. That's the perfect scenario. You want to win a Stanley Cup. You want to play 1,000 games. Those were things I wanted to achieve, but I wasn't able to. I think I could have played 1,000 games had I not been forced to retire because of my concussions.

I totaled exactly 300 points in my NHL career. It's not a big number, but I look back now and wish I had fought a little less and scored a little more, because I think I could have been in the 500-point range, but I chose my path, and I'm very happy with the career I had in the NHL. I loved being the center of attention, and the fighting made me a fan favorite on some of these teams. I loved entertaining. I loved being the focal point.

I was a good third-line winger. When coaches had me as the tough guy, I got fourth-line duties, didn't play much, and was in the penalty box for fighting, so that drastically cut into my production. But I am very thankful and was well compensated for the role I played on those teams. It made me a lot of money. I was able to do a little bit of both—scoring and fighting. Having said that, I could have put up more points had I not had to be the heavyweight on so many of the teams I played for.

I never went into a season thinking I was going to lead the league in penalty minutes, but I have to admit that at the end of a season, if I was close to leading the NHL in penalty minutes, I'd want to get it. It was part of my game. It's not like winning a scoring title, but there is some pride in knowing I stood up for my teammates. And opponents knew that I was willing to do anything for my team. I collected 2,562 minutes in penalty through my regular-season career. As of this writing, I am 18th on the list of the NHL's all-time penalty leaders. I don't know whether that's something to be proud of, but I must admit that I am. Hey, I'm in the record book for something!

I look back at the places where I had the most success: Buffalo, New York, and Colorado. The one common denominator was that in each of those cities, we had other guys to face the heavyweights. I didn't have to fight every night. In Buffalo we had Rob Ray and Brad May. They were my security blankets to fight the Stu Grimsons and Tony Twists. I never had to look over my shoulder when I stepped onto the ice. I could play my game and if I wanted to fight Stu Grimson, I could, but I didn't have to. There is a big difference. In New York we had Sandy McCarthy, Steve McKenna, Dale Purinton, and Chris Simon, so I got to play and my points went up. In Colorado we had Jim Cummins and Peter Worrell, so again I got to play my game. But when I first went to Pittsburgh, I was the only guy. When the heavyweights on the other team came onto the ice, I constantly had to look over my shoulder. It doesn't matter who you are, those boys are tough sons of bitches. When you're looking over your shoulder, it's hard to concentrate on the offensive side of the game. When I went to Tampa Bay, again I was the only guy, so I didn't score. In Chicago I was the only guy who fought, and it was the same when I went to Dallas. I had to fight all the heavies. There's a correlation. I played at 188 pounds. When I had other guys who'd fight, I was a much better player.

Ending my playing career was a relief right away. For one thing, I didn't have to fight anymore. I didn't have to lay awake before a game wondering who I was going to have to fight and wondering if I was going to get injured. Hockey fights are not orchestrated. Guys are trying to hurt each other. Was I going to have my jaw broken or my orbital bone broken?

But while ending my playing career was a relief in some ways, the finality was also crushing. Playing in the NHL was all that I ever wanted to do. I didn't have anything to fall back on. I quit school when I was playing Junior—I was going to make a career of playing hockey. I did what young players shouldn't do, which is put all their eggs in one basket, but it worked out for me.

Everyone identifies you as a hockey player. I played since I was five years old, and all of a sudden, I wasn't going to be playing anymore. I loved the fans cheering me on, I loved my name being chanted from the stands, I loved seeing the signs held up by fans and the jerseys with my name and number on the back. Leaving that part is hard. Plus, my kids were young and they didn't get to see me play very much.

In the sports industry, very few plan for life after hockey. If you are thinking about retirement, it's over. You're done. I hadn't thought about life after hockey for a single second until my last year. Up until then, it was going 100 miles per hour as a hockey player. When I got bought out by Chicago, I realized that I could be one year away from doing nothing. I knew I was done during that last season when I started looking at my cell phone between periods to check up on my kids and to see if my eight-year-old son had won his games and if he had scored in them.

So I started to think about new career possibilities. I was only 34 years old, and I always knew I was a good interview. TV work was certainly something I thought I could do. I enjoy talking, I know the game, and I am very opinionated. I'm not afraid to say what I think, so I thought it might be an avenue I'd like to explore.

During what ended up being my final season, after Dallas was knocked out of the playoffs, the Score in Toronto reached out to me at playoff time to do daily hits on their network. I did them from a TV station in Dallas.

When I returned to Buffalo, I played a bit of golf, but I got bored. It was only about a month until Steve Dryden from TSN called me and asked if I would be interested in doing a few evenings talking about games still being played. It was seamless. I'd sit and watch the game and one of the hosts would ask me a question and I'd respond. It was simple, and I wasn't afraid to call out guys if needed. I just gave a fair examination of the game we were watching. While I was working pretty regularly for TSN, I got a call from a guy at ESPN telling me that Barry Melrose was leaving to return to coaching and asked whether I would be interested in interviewing for that job. He explained that there would be an interview process. I had never interviewed for a job in my life! I had just started in broadcasting, and ESPN was big time.

When I showed up, I asked how many were competing for the gig. I was told 40! Some had a great deal of experience. I didn't think I stood a chance. It was a grueling process. We started at 8:00 in the morning and met an executive every half hour until noon. After lunch, we did on-camera work, going through highlight packets, and then met more executives until 4:00. After that, I went to the hotel and flew home the next day. And then I waited. A month later I got a call and was told that I got the job. I signed a three-year contract with them.

I didn't really know what I was doing. I was just watching hockey and commenting. The one thing I wanted to avoid was saying "um" or any of those crutch words and phrases, so I made a conscious decision to shorten my sentences and avoid the crutches. I loved ESPN, but they weren't rights holders when I was there. There was very little hockey. It was all football, baseball, and basketball. The people there were great. It was a well-oiled media machine. Sometimes I'd watch all of these games, but then they'd throw to me and I'd be on for a matter of seconds. As much as I loved it, it could be quite boring. If it was hockey, all they wanted to hear about was Alex Ovechkin and Sidney Crosby. There could be a million great games going on, but they only wanted Ovechkin and Crosby. In Canada hockey is religion. I was making notes on fourth liners with the Canucks and they wanted Ovechkin and Crosby, even if they didn't play that night. But it was an awesome time, and I learned a lot. I look back now and wonder how bad I must have been. I wasn't nervous, but I was overprepared for what ESPN was. I love being in front of the camera. Love being on the radio. I've made lifelong friends with so many great people I've met through the broadcasting profession.

At the same time, I was also coaching my son. All I did was coach Matthew and work. I know it's a difficult transition for a lot of guys who don't know what they're going to do when their career is over, but It was a pretty easy transition for me.

I love structure. I love waking up at 7:30 and having an itinerary laid out for the day. I don't do well without structure. That's where a lot of guys get into trouble. They don't know what they're going to do from day to day. And for the first time since they were eight years old, they have no structure to their lives.

* * *

The Sabres Carnival was an event for fans started by the wives of the team in 1980 as a way to raise funds for charity. It was an annual tradition. There were a lot of things going on, but the fans could line up and meet their favorite players, and that is where I met a beautiful young girl named Christine Cardarella. She was there with her fiancé, and they were both friends with Rob Ray. I joked and asked if she had a sister for me, and we all laughed.

I would occasionally see Christine at Razor's when the team went out for a drink. We flirted a little bit, and by then, she and her fiancé had split up. We ended up going for lunch and dinner and started dating.

She was a very pretty girl, and I loved her, but I was equally attracted to her family, as I said before, and that translated into wanting to be a father and have a family of my own.

Christine and I got married in Buffalo, her hometown, on June 29, 1997, and we went to Hawaii for our honeymoon. We had two great kids and raised them the way I had always imagined. Christine was a terrific wife and a terrific mom to our two children.

After I retired, we returned to Buffalo. Hockey players are on the road a lot, and you don't fully understand your relationship until you are with your partner day in and day out. I retired at the age of 35, and our marriage unfolded quickly. I am the one to blame for our relationship not working out. Christine never wanted to get divorced, and that was my doing. It was the hardest thing I ever went through, in part because our two kids were involved.

Christine is an amazing mother to our kids, Matthew and Taylor. She is very disciplined and organized and insists on respect. I don't think there is a person in the world who is as aligned with me on how to raise our children. I can now talk to Christine as a friend, and do so almost every day, because we love our kids together more than anything in this world. There is no one I could have wished to raise kids with more than my ex-wife.

Christine and I were going through a divorce and arguing a great deal, mostly about money. After we split up, Christine started seeing another guy right away. He was much younger than her. Because I love my kids as much as I do, having another man around caused a lot of challenges. I resented the guy. My jealousy kicked in, but an even bigger point of contention was that I didn't want another guy around my kids. That was the hardest part for me. I had some verbal jabs back and forth with this guy. I told him I didn't care what he and Christine did, but he was to stay away from our kids. He sent me a long text message that asked how I was going to like it when he tucked my kids into bed. Anyone who knows me knows that I am the wrong person to send a text like that to.

I was working at ESPN in May 2011 and had taken a day off so I could take Taylor to her third-grade father/daughter dance. It was really important to me. That afternoon, I was hanging out with my buddies and had a few drinks before I was to take Taylor to the dance. Christine called me and asked me where I was because I was going to be late picking up our daughter. There had been a miscommunication about the time. The dance started an hour earlier than I had originally been told. Already upset, I hurried over to the house, and Christine's boyfriend was there. I was still fuming about his text message, so we started yelling at each other. He chirped at me and I challenged him to step outside.

In my rage, I was yelling obscenities while I kicked in the garage door. I was livid! I still owned the house, but I was wrong to do that, and I am quick to admit it. Christine called the police. I left, but when the police arrived at the house and got the statement, they had to go out and get me. I was taken back to the house. Christine pleaded with the cops to let me go. She had called 9-1-1 because she was afraid. I think she was more afraid of what I might do to the guy she was with. She told the cops repeatedly that I hadn't touched her.

I never laid a hand on Christine—never once through our relationship—but in the United States, you can be charged with domestic violence without touching a person. I ended up getting arrested. Because I entered the garage, the cops told me I could also be charged with breaking and entering.

I was charged with criminal mischief, trespassing, harassment, contempt, and aggravated harassment and accused of causing about $300 in damage to the garage door. I pled not guilty to felony criminal mischief, and the district attorney ordered me to complete 500 hours of community service to have the charges dropped. I was also issued a one-year order of protection from Christine and was barred from taking any "offensive" action against her and ordered to avoid contact with her boyfriend. I also had to attend anger-management counseling. The misdemeanor charges of criminal mischief and aggravated harassment were dropped. Christine dumped the boyfriend the day after the incident.

Although all the charges were dropped, I had an open file on my record. I had to go a year without getting into trouble. Because I was on probation, I could cross the border into Canada, but I couldn't get back into the States. As a result, I couldn't take a chance on visiting my mother in Ottawa, but even bigger for me was that I coached my son's hockey team and we played in Canada a lot.

On December 11, 2011, I was at the Ale House in Cheektowaga with some buddies watching the football game. The New York Giants were playing the Dallas Cowboys. After the game, I talked to my son, who was with his team playing in a tournament in Hamilton, Ontario. Matthew was so excited. "Daddy, I scored the winner in overtime and we won the championship!" he said.

I could hear the elation in his voice. I congratulated him, told him how proud of him I was and that I loved him. I was so full of joy for his success, but as I left the bar to go home, I pulled over and burst into tears. Happy tears, but then it struck me that I was supposed to be there with Matthew and the team, and my happy tears turned to tears of rage. I couldn't be there because of the stupid situation I had gotten into earlier in the year. Instead of going home, I went downtown and proceeded to drink away my sadness. I drank and drank and drank and drank.

That night I had committed to attend an event called Catwalk for Charity that the Buffalo Sabres held every year. It was a high-end fashion show for charity. A lot of the players were there. I remember doing shots at the bar with Zack Kassian, who played with Buffalo in 2011–12. While I was there, Ville Leino, who played on that same Sabres team, confronted me about comments I had made about him on ESPN. I said he was overpaid and he started pointing a finger in my face. He was challenging me, and I'd finally had enough. I pushed him away. Zack Kassian said, "He's not worth it," and we continued to drink. The sadness had just enveloped me.

I drank to get drunk that evening. It was the only time in my life I ever did that. I drank to obliterate what I had missed.

It was time to get out of there. I don't even remember getting into my car. I couldn't even walk. Someone should have grabbed my keys. I got into my Porsche Cayenne and started to drive home, which was about 30 miles away from where I lived. I was so hammered that I couldn't see straight. As I was driving, I hit a guardrail and lost a wheel, but I continued driving and ended up driving about nine miles on three wheels! Sparks were flying off the rim as it scraped against the asphalt! People were calling the cops reporting a guy driving down the road on three wheels!

Seven troopers were following behind me, and they finally got me pulled over not far from my house. The cops found me driving my car with damage to the front end and missing a front tire. I refused to take a Breathalyzer and was arrested on the spot and had my license revoked. Thank God I didn't hurt anyone. I was lucky. If I had blown into the Breathalyzer, I'm told that my reactions indicated I'd likely have blown a 3.5, which is roughly five times the legal limit. It was definitely a learning experience.

I embarrassed my kids and I lost my job at ESPN. It was a really rough time for me. Two days later, I pled guilty to driving while intoxicated, refusing a breath test, driving with unsafe tires, and failing to notify the Department of Motor Vehicles of my change of address. I had to pay a $1,950 fine, attend alcohol-abuse counseling, and perform 100 hours of community service.

* * *

While I was going through my divorce, I had all kinds of different emotions. During that time, I met a beautiful young hostess. Amber Lindke had been crowned Miss Buffalo in 2007. I was crazy about her, although there was a substantial age gap. I was 35 and she was 21.

Amber and I had an affair in 2012, and for some reason I asked her to marry me, and we got engaged. I bought her a $50,000 engagement ring. Candidly, I was at a low point in my life, and having a beautiful girl show me attention was really attractive to me, although in retrospect I can now say that I wasn't in love with Amber. I guess I was searching for something.

We moved in together, but it wasn't long before I realized that I didn't want to marry Amber. She was too young and we had nothing in common. And it didn't help that my kids didn't like her. We broke up.

At the time, I still didn't have my license, so Amber was driving my Cadillac Escalade. I asked for the car and the ring back and offered to give her some money so she could get on her feet, but she refused. "Fuck you. I want the car and I want the ring," she said. I told her that there was no way that was going to happen.

I contacted my lawyer, and he got in touch with Amber's lawyer. It was her and her lawyer's position that she was entitled to the ring and the car, but my lawyer knew otherwise. "No, she isn't entitled to either, and you know it," he said. Instead they asked for a lump sum of $10,000, but I had my back up and said I'd give her $2,000. They came back with a counteroffer, but I said, "No way." Amber then threatened to take the story to the media, knowing that I didn't want my name back in the press again, but I said, "If you think that is going to scare me, go right ahead." She did, and the papers ran with the story. But if you want to see stubborn, I have STUBBORN tattooed on my ass, as well as DETERMINED, PASSIONATE, FEARLESS, and HONEST. I dug in my heels. No one is going to bully me!

I got the ring back and the car and ended up giving her $1,000. I wanted to pay her with pennies, but my lawyer warned me against that. It was a crazy back-and-forth negotiation. It is always fun when you know you're going to win and that the other side doesn't stand a chance. The case never even went before a judge. Under New York law, the person who received an engagement ring is required to give it back if the relationship goes south before marriage, regardless of whose actions might have caused the breakup.

*   *   *

When I first moved to Quebec City to play Junior, I billeted with the Robitaille family. Veronique Robitaille, the daughter, later reached out to me on social media and we renewed our friendship. I went to Quebec City a few times to visit her and had a really great time. She is a really nice girl, and a relationship began.

A few months later, Veronique decided to go back to work. That posed all kinds of problems. I was living in Buffalo and she lived and worked in Quebec City. I wasn't going to move to Quebec, and she wasn't going to move to Buffalo. It simply wasn't going to work. We had to make some decisions. What did we have to do if we were going to make a go of things? Veronique decided she would move to Buffalo. The only thing we could do to get her into the United States was to get married. It was a piece of paper, a formality. We got married in 2014, but it didn't work out. We were too similar, both with fiery temperaments. It's unfortunate, because Veronique is a really nice girl.

A couple years later, I was attending a fundraising event in Ottawa. A guy I knew had gone out with his buddies on his 40th birthday and ended up flipping his golf cart and broke his neck. I hadn't heard about it at the time and only found out when an acquaintance asked if I could donate something for a fundraiser that was being held for him. I contacted every team I had played for and they all donated jerseys, which I signed, to be used as auction items at the event. The organizers asked if I could attend, and I told them I would try, but I also had committed to a number of things that my kids were involved in. As it turned out, at the same time as the event, my son was going to a tryout with the Pembroke Lumber Kings, a Tier Two Junior A team. As Pembroke is not that far from Ottawa, I was able to attend the fundraiser, and I stayed with my cousin, who lived close to where the benefit was being held.

After I left Ottawa to play Junior, I hadn't spent much time there except to visit my mother, so I saw people I hadn't seen in 20 years. One of the event organizers was Debbie Hershorn, who was a great friend of mine when I was growing up. She asked, "Have you seen Rhonda?" Rhonda was a girl I had dated when we were younger, but I hadn't seen her since we broke up 23 years earlier. About 10 minutes later, I ran into Rhonda, and we fell into conversation like we hadn't missed a beat. We spent the evening reminiscing and catching up on life—her three kids and my two kids. And we've been together ever since. She's a fabulous girl, and we have a terrific life together.

Just when I thought everything in my life had fallen nicely into place, I ran into trouble again in March 2020. I went to Nashville for an NHL charity event. It was a tournament, so I thought I would extend my time there so I could see my son play a couple of league games. One was in Evansville, Indiana, and the other was in Huntsville, Alabama, and in between, Rhonda and I could hang out in Nashville, a city that we love.

We rented an Airbnb. Rhonda flew in to meet me, and the first night she was there, we went to Kid Rock's Big Ass Honky Tonk & Rock 'n' Roll Steakhouse for a few drinks, watched a live band, and then went over to Nashville Crossroads and listened to some more live music there. We sat at the bar on the third floor, having a great time, telling stories and laughing and kibitzing with our bartender, who was so sweet. I put my hand gently on Rhonda's throat in the context of some story, and we were laughing, and out of nowhere, a woman I hadn't seen came over and told Rhonda, "You don't have to put up with that!" Rhonda told her, "No, no, no. We are just having fun! It's all good! I'm not uncomfortable." Then the woman started poking her finger into my chest, yelling at me. I was stunned! I looked over at the males sitting at her table and said, "Get her the fuck out of my face!"

One of the guys had words with me and then everything went to shit. Out of the corner of my eye, I saw four bouncers come flying in at me. I put my left arm out to protect myself trying to hold them off, and we ended up on the floor.

We were on the third floor and I was pulled down the stairs, which were incredibly steep, and dragged out of the bar by the bouncers. Rhonda had her arms pinned back and they were pulling her down the stairs too. She dug her feet in and begged them to let her walk out of the bar on her own so that she didn't get hurt. She was really afraid! They finally let her walk out of the bar.

We got out to the street and the cops were there. I was so mad! I didn't even know why I was there being pushed into a paddy wagon! Rhonda begged to tell our side of the story, and the police didn't want to hear a word that she had to say. They heard the bouncers' side of the story but didn't want to hear our side.

I was so embarrassed. I didn't do anything, and there I was spending the night in jail. I didn't sleep all night. At 8:00 they let me out. You have to stay for a set number of hours before you are released. I was charged with public intoxication and assault on a bouncer at the bar during the scrap. I was livid! I never choked a bouncer! I didn't even know why I had been arrested and thrown into jail!

I Googled "Nashville lawyers," phoned one, and left a message. In the meantime, I called Bill Daly at the NHL's head office and a few other people to explain what had happened and ask for their advice. The lawyer called me back and kind of chuckled. "Tourist," he said. I asked him what he meant. He said, "This happens all the time. I can already tell you how this is going to go down. There's a template. If you write a check to the bar for $1,500, everything will be dropped. You can fight it, but you have to remember that the people who own the bars in Nashville are in with top political people and the police. You can come back here to Nashville once or twice, pay to fly here and rent a hotel room. You can spend that money with no promise that you'll win this case. Or you can write a check for $1,500 and it's done. I can't tell you how many times I've been through this same scenario."

I wrote the check the next week, and it was done. Everything was dropped. Of course, the fact that everything was dropped never got into the media, but the arrest sure did. I never choked a bouncer and never even got into a fight. It's a racket.

We left Nashville and drove to Huntsville to watch Matthew play. He scored his first professional hat trick that night. What did Charles Dickens write in *A Tale of Two Cities*? "It was the worst of times; it was the best of times." Something like that.

CHAPTER 18

THE BEAR AND THE PRINCESS

MY KIDS ARE MY EVERYTHING. I know most people identify Matthew Barnaby as a hockey player, and I understand that. I never refer to myself in that way. When I meet people, I say, "Nice to meet you. I'm Matthew." Sometimes I get, "I know you from somewhere." Sometimes they figure it out, but most times, they are left with a puzzled look, thinking, *Did he go to the same high school as me? Or did I see him at the gym? Maybe he's just got one of those recognizable faces.* It's just not me to live in the past; I'm always looking to the future.

I'm very proud to have played in the NHL, but it doesn't define me. What does define me is being father to Matthew and Taylor. I think it's the single most important thing I can do. I didn't have a father in my life, so I want to make sure that my kids feel loved and supported, and know that no matter what, I am always there for them.

Matthew, our firstborn, was born on May 2, 1998. He's a mini-me in every way. He's cocky, funny, and just a really great kid. But there is one difference: Matthew is 6'3"! I was a small kid at 15 and grew at 16, and Matthew was a late developer too. In fact, he developed even later than I did, but he grew three inches at the age of 20.

I have a really close bond with my son. He loves sports just like I did. He's a great golfer and baseball player, and a very talented hockey player. Matthew loves hockey more than anyone I know. Between improving his play, working out, and studying hockey plays on YouTube, you won't find anyone as determined to have a career in hockey.

I loved coaching Matthew, but if he was going to attempt to make a career out of hockey, he needed further training. When he was 17, we sent him to Avon Old Farms, a private prep school in Connecticut where Brian Leetch had been going when he was drafted by the Rangers. It was a terrific experience for Matthew. After Avon we moved him up to Canada, and in 2016–17, he played Junior A for the Pembroke Lumber Kings. I was able to watch him fairly regularly. In his second year, he scored 32 goals and had 76 points and played in the All-Star Game. Then in 2018–19 he joined the Chicago Steel in the USHL. It's a great league, but Matthew was only getting to play three or four minutes per game, so we asked for a trade, and he was dealt to the Youngstown Phantoms in the same league. That was a much better place for Matthew to continue his development. He went to the Toronto Maple Leafs rookie camp in 2018–19, and that was a great experience. In 2021–22, he played for the Fort Wayne Komets of the East Coast Hockey League.

I love watching his journey. My son is a much better hockey player than I ever was. He has 10 times the mouth too! Getting someone to give him a chance has been the hardest thing. His resilience to battle through every level when no one but his mom and I believed in him has been amazing. Matthew is trying to move up in the crazy world of hockey, where there are a lot of ups and downs. I don't give a shit whether he gets to play in the NHL. I just want him to continue doing something he loves.

Taylor is our second child, and she came into the world on July 23, 2001. She is beautiful, smart, funny, and very strong. I hope some of her traits come from me, but I must admit that she really is her mom.

Taylor tried to play sports. She played soccer and softball, and neither worked out, but damn—she was always the cutest on the field. With her hair in a ponytail, those pink cleats always matched her pink jersey and accentuated her bubbly personality. During the couple of years that

Taylor played sports, she almost kicked the soccer ball once, and on one occasion, she came close to hitting the softball. When I saw that she was struggling, I made her a deal: I'd give her $400 to spend at the mall if she would give up playing soccer and softball. For a little girl who loves clothes, that decision was a no-brainer!

Dance was a different story. Five days a week, Taylor took dance lessons: ballet, modern, lyrical—you name it, she did it. I loved going to her dance competitions. As much as Matthew made me proud on the ice, watching my baby girl dance made me equally proud. Most of her performances or competitions ended with me in a puddle of tears.

Taylor moved to New York City to continue to pursue dance at the age of 15, but she came to realize that New York wasn't for her. The prospect of not eating and with earning potential quite low, she had had enough. She was very mature at a young age and has never looked back. She is now attending John Carroll University in Ohio studying human resources. I am so proud of her. She is an amazing young lady.

What I've come to realize is that it doesn't matter what my kids choose to do with their lives as long as they are happy and safe. Everything I do is for my kids. There are a lot of challenges in being a parent, but when it comes down to it, there is no greater love. Anyone who doesn't have kids can never fully comprehend the love you have for your children. When they go through things, you hurt more than they do. I just want to be the best possible dad that I can be. They make me a better person. I want them always to know how special they are and want them to know how loved they are every day.

I tear up when I talk about my kids. I've made a lot of mistakes in life, but I always tried my hardest to be a great father. I grew up without a father, so being a really great parent is very important to me. I probably need to thank Dwayne Hewston, my biological father, for this, because while I have never thought of him, he has made me want to be a great dad to my children. I hope I've succeeded.

CHAPTER 19

YOU CAN TAKE THE MAN OUT OF HOCKEY, BUT YOU CAN'T TAKE THE HOCKEY OUT OF THE MAN

ALTHOUGH MY NHL CAREER ENDED, I never left hockey. I love hockey so much, and I have always been a student of the game. I love breaking down plays.

I was likely a little over the top when I was coaching my son from the time he was young. I coached his teams too. Even when I was coaching 10-year-olds, I was breaking down video with them. It is the best tool in the world. Every couple of weeks, I'd have a parent film the game and we'd go over a period with the kids. It doesn't matter whether you are 10 or playing in the NHL, you learn from mistakes, so I'd pick out one mistake and we'd talk about it. Everybody thinks they are doing things right, but when you see it, you realize it and you can correct it.

I've coached a lot through the years, and some of the kids I've coached have gone on to college, some to Junior, and some to the NHL. That's great, but having the chance to play a role in their lives between the ages of 10 to 17—those are important years—and helping them grow not only as hockey players but as people are the most important things to me.

I get really emotional when I receive pictures from kids I've coached, showing what they're doing today. Being a part of their development is so wonderful to me. I cherish the times I had working with the kids, having fun with them, and having fun with the parents. It's one of the things I miss a lot.

I loved coaching kids. There are two things that are important to me: One is holding people accountable, not just in hockey but in life. We live in a soft world, and kids get away with things and the blame is often put on the coach, the teacher, or the parent. The other thing is helping make the kids not only the best hockey players they can be but the best *people* they can be.

I coached my son, Matthew, until it was important that he get coached by other people. You are always hardest on your own kid when you're coaching. I knew that if I was hardest on him, no parent could ever question if I was hard on their son or the amount of ice time Matthew got.

After Matthew moved on, I was out of coaching for a year. Then my former teammate with Buffalo Jay McKee, who knew what I had done in coaching, asked me if I was interested in assisting him with the Kitchener Rangers of the Ontario Hockey League for the 2016–17 season. I respect Jay as much as anyone as a player and as a person. We were teammates in Buffalo from 1995–96 to 1998–99. We even reunited as teammates for some fun with the Dundas Real McCoys playing Senior hockey during the 2013–14 season. We won the Allan Cup that season. I wasn't looking for a position when Jay offered me one, and I was happy with what I was doing working in the media, but I thought working with Jay in Kitchener would be a really interesting and unique challenge.

"I am very excited and feel very fortunate to welcome Matthew Barnaby to my staff, and to the Kitchener Rangers family," Jay McKee said in the June 2016 media release that announced my hiring. I responded, "I am so excited to be joining the Kitchener Rangers. I look forward to working with a lot of great young players and helping them improve and achieve their dreams. I want to thank the management and coaching staff for this amazing opportunity to be a part of a great team and storied franchise."

Kitchener had an excellent season the year before with Mike Van Ryn as the head coach, finishing sixth overall, but the London Knights ended their season in the quarterfinal. Mike resigned in May 2016, and Jay was hired as head coach and brought me on board to look after the defense—the defensive side is so important.

Some people wondered what kind of a coach I could be and what kind of influence I would have on players, judging me by the way I played in the NHL. I was a totally different Matthew Barnaby than the player was. I was a lot more passive, teaching and talking, than the idiot I sometimes was when I was on the ice. I didn't care what people thought. It didn't matter to me. I love having fun, and while I was teaching the players, we were always laughing.

I am 18th all-time on the NHL's penalty leaders list, and there I was in Kitchener, with Jay McKee, teaching discipline to young players. But if you look at the players on that list of penalty leaders—Chris Chelios, Dale Hunter, Scott Stevens—they're all guys like me who put the team first. I wanted the guys to stand up for their teammates but in a smart way.

Being a coach is essentially the same as being a teacher. You don't get the best out of a student if you're screaming and yelling at them. You teach them what you want, and if they make the same mistakes over and over, you have to show them a different way. You show them the good things they do and what they need to improve.

These kids were better than we were at that age. There was more skill taught on a daily basis. These kids were going through a lot of changes in their lives. There was a lot more pressure on them, and that growth was part of the job that made it fun. I always looked forward to watching the guys grow and seeing what they'd look like as players and people in three or four years.

I can't say that I loved spending my life on buses again. But as an athlete, there's nothing greater than the feeling of winning—that in-game chess match of trying to figure out how to win. We lived for game day, and we loved it when we were playing, being in the fire. I loved watching the boys with that same fire that I had.

We finished with a record of 36 wins, 27 losses, and five overtime losses for 77 points, good for sixth in the Western Conference in 2016–17, but we were knocked out by Owen Sound in the first round of the playoffs. That Nick Suzuki isn't a bad player!

I was really enthusiastic about the 2017–18 season. Jay and I had a year of experience under our belts. Riley Damiani was one of our key forwards, and we added Logan Stanley, a 6'7" defenseman, in a trade with the Windsor Spitfires. Damiani was the AHL's Rookie of the Year in 2020–21, leading all AHL rookies in scoring and tying for third overall in the scoring race. He made his NHL debut with the Dallas Stars in 2021–22. Logan Stanley joined the Winnipeg Jets during the 2020–21 NHL season and is now a key part of their defense.

Mike McKenzie, the son of hockey insider Bob McKenzie, had been named general manager of the team in March 2017. I don't think Mike wanted either Jay or me there. We weren't his guys. Just like anywhere else, the new general manager wants to bring in his own people. That's just part of sports at all levels when you get past youth. I can't say that I saw eye to eye with Mike. I don't think he's a bad guy, but we had different philosophies on coaching. Let's just say our personalities didn't mesh. I ended up losing that job but not because Jay McKee wanted me gone. He thought he was going to lose me at some point to be a head coach in the OHL.

Near the end of training camp in September 2017, I was out for dinner with Rhonda. We went for a few drinks after dinner, and after our first drink, we saw four or five of our players out at the same bar where we were. It was about a quarter to 11:00 by then, and curfew was at 11:00. I told my girlfriend, "We've got to leave here." All the players were of drinking age. There was no underage drinking, and I am not the kind of guy to tattle on the players for missing curfew. I reminded the players that curfew was at 11:00, and my girlfriend and I left, so in theory the boys could have gone home in the next 15 minutes. That was the end of it. At least I thought so.

We had an open rule: If you're drinking, you don't drive. Take a taxi or an Uber and bring me a receipt and you'll have your money reimbursed, no questions asked. I had made the mistake of drinking and driving in the past, and there was no way I wanted our guys or *anyone* to drink and drive. A few days later, one of the guys I'd seen at the bar came to me with a receipt. I turned it in to the general manager without looking at it. I just figured they were out for some beers and did the responsible thing, but the time on the receipt was between 2:15 and 2:30 in the morning. The players got called into the office and admitted they were out after curfew.

I was brought in and asked if I knew the players were out that night. I admitted that I had seen them at 10:45 and then left, so that was all I could speak to. I hadn't said a word because I wanted to retain the trust of the players. I was let go. At the time, Mike McKenzie said it was because of "philosophical differences" but did not want to "get into the nitty-gritty of it."

The guys on the team said that they were not going to play as a result. They were standing up for me, but I told them, "Guys, this is your career. As much as I love coaching you and being part of this team, this is not the end of the world on my end. You guys have to keep playing. This is your shot."

I had a tough conversation with Jay McKee. He's still one of my best friends. I still talk to him three or four times a week. Jay is a great coach, a great human being, and a great family man. He had a fantastic season with Kitchener in 2017–18, finishing first in their division and second in the conference. They went to the Western Conference Final but lost to the Soo Greyhounds in double overtime in the deciding seventh game. I was pleased for Jay and happy for the team, but I knew that he was next. Mike McKenzie fired Jay in November 2019, and he is now the coach and general manager. Jay landed on his feet and is now head coach of the Hamilton Bulldogs.

Going to work with Jay every day was amazing. To coach at that level was a great learning experience, and it was so much fun. Everybody on the team wanted to play in the NHL. The reality is that few are going to achieve that dream, but they are eager and are sponges to learn more that will help them advance their careers. I absolutely loved my time there. The Kitchener Rangers are an unbelievable organization.

The Ontario Hockey League is an awesome league, and Kitchener is an amazing place. For the kids, playing in front of 7,000 fans each night is just incredible. Having said that, I would never go back to coaching Junior hockey. Even though I was one of the highest-paid assistant coaches in the league, making $80,000 a year, I have no desire to go back to riding a bus through the night all over Ontario. It was an awesome experience, but I am much happier with my life today. I have an ideal situation now. I can work out of my home, enjoy time with my girlfriend, travel, work at BET99.net, and be involved in fundraising events where I can meet people and help raise money for important causes.

And I don't have to ride a bus to Sault Ste. Marie.

CHAPTER 20

I'LL GIVE YOU 10-TO-1 ODDS

WHEN I WAS YOUNG, our family lived next to relatives, and every Friday night, my mom would go over there to play poker. They played betting quarters and 50 cents, and the most anyone could lose was $10. When I was 10 years old, I earned money cutting grass, and I'd take my money and get into the poker game with them. They'd let me play, and if I lost, they took my money.

I was a gambler from the time I was young. I loved the adrenaline of betting. I'd shoot basketballs with buddies to see who could get the most hoops, and the winner would get five bucks. We'd play double or nothing until somebody took home all the cash. When I was 13 and 14 years old, I often came home with a couple hundred dollars from a poker game or some other form of betting. We didn't have money as a family, but if I had 10 dollars in my pocket, I was looking for a way to make 20. I lived in a housing development, and my mom and brother would just laugh and shake their heads. They knew how much I loved betting.

When I went to the NHL and was making real money for the first time, we'd be flying someplace on a road trip, and there'd be a group of guys who would be at the back of the plane playing cards. I was 19 years old when I got called up to Buffalo. Dave Hannan, Pat LaFontaine, Brad May, Wayne Presley, and Petr Svoboda would be playing poker, and I asked if I could join them. The buy-in was $500. If you lost, you could lose a couple thousand dollars, but you could also win a couple thousand. I was a little nervous because this was real money. After our first road trip flying to a couple of cities, I was up about $4,500. *Holy fuck, I am breaking these guys*, I thought.

I was living in the Hilton in downtown Buffalo for a couple months. I was a stupid 19-year-old kid. I bought a 52-inch TV for my hotel room. On the next road trip, I lost four grand. I asked, "Does anybody want a 52-inch TV?" They said, "No, we'll take the cash." It was quite a learning moment for me.

When I was in Pittsburgh, we had huge poker games there. Tom Barrasso, Rob Brown, and Jaromir Jagr, who is one of the biggest gamblers I've ever seen in my life. These guys played for gigantic pots of $20,000, $30,000, $40,000. No one likes to lose that kind of money, and it can affect your play when you are losing money like that, especially with teammates.

I was playing a game called Follow the Queen with Tommy Barrasso and a few of the boys. If you know the game, you know that there are a lot of good hands out there. There was roughly $12,000 in the pot. There was a rule that you had to have the cash or a check on you. It was Tommy's bet, but he looked at me and said he didn't have the cash on him, but I knew he was good for the money. Tommy drove a different Ferrari to work every day. If you asked him where he got it, he'd tell you that you weren't rich enough to afford one.

At the poker table, he looked at me and asked, "Can I put my watch in if I lose?" It was a Patek Philippe worth something like $10,000. I fucking love watches because I could never afford one when I was younger. I was fine with that. "No problem at all!" I said. I knew that my hand couldn't be beaten. I was sitting there with a royal flush, but he must have had a good hand too. He laid his hand down and I turned over my cards, and he handed me his Patek Philippe. Tommy was the kind of guy you wanted to win from. I love Tommy Barrasso;

he doesn't hide who he is. But no one loves Tommy Barrasso more than Tommy Barrasso!

If I could pick one ideal job to do in this world, it would be a poker player. I absolutely love it, and I can play for days on end without sleep. Winning at poker isn't luck. It takes great skill and strategy. There is a reason guys such as my friend Daniel Negreanu, one of the best poker players in the world, win over and over again. He has won six World Series of Poker bracelets and two World Poker Tour championships. As I have learned, and seen it reinforced by Daniel, success in life is when preparation and hard work are added to a little bit of luck.

I like to bet on the golf course for large sums of money. That's another of my favorite things, but I try to find a guy who I can have an advantage over. If I'm a seven handicap and he's a seven handicap but I know I'm better than him, I want to play him for as much money as possible. If I'm playing a guy and we're both a seven handicap and I know he's three times better than me, then I want my three shots. I like to believe that 99 out of 100 bets in golf are won on the first tee. Either you're better than your opponent and you know it or he's a fish—someone who is inexperienced or just not very good. There's a saying: "If you don't know who the fish is, you're the fish."

I used to bet on football with Jaromir Jagr. Everybody had a bookie back then, and we were no different. On Tuesdays you'd collect your money or pay your debt from betting. That was just the way it worked. I've always enjoyed football, and betting on football has never affected my lifestyle. I've always played with what I can afford to lose. Sometimes you lose four or five thousand dollars in a week and sometimes you win four or five thousand. Back in the day, I didn't do any research. I just picked teams I liked or thought could win. I was playing hockey at the time, so it was all for fun.

I've always loved gambling. Betting enhances the enjoyment you get out of the game. But as always, you have to play within your means. You don't gamble to pay bills. You don't gamble to feed your family.

If you have an addictive personality or can't control yourself, it's not something you want to involve yourself in. You gamble for enjoyment.

Legalized gambling has created a giant footprint, and I now work for a great company called BET99.net, an online Canadian gambling site. BET99 followed what I was doing on Twitter, thought I was very knowledgeable in various sports, liked my reasoning, and offered me a position, so now it's a job. I still bet on football and hockey, but now I'm more into baseball, basketball, and even soccer. I get up in the morning and look at trends, the over/under, and where I can find value. I watch the teams play. It's easy to say one team is going to beat another, but if it's going to cost you $300 to win $100, that's a terrible bet. I don't always go with the flashiest games because those might be the hardest ones to pick, but I go for the games in which I think I have an advantage. I really research, going through all the numbers. Just like in poker, math is the most important component in betting.

I'll bet on hockey, NFL football, college football, NBA basketball, college basketball, and baseball. You have to do a lot of research when you're gambling the kind of money I play with. I'm a thrill seeker. I love the action. But you bet what you can afford to lose. That's the main thing. I do it for pleasure and as a job, but I also don't risk money that will affect my lifestyle. I have a saying I adhere to: A gambling dollar has no home. You might win one day but you'll lose another day.

You have to bet responsibly. I love working with Bet99. They let me be myself. I study a lot and spend a lot of time picking games. I pass along educated guesses to those who enjoy betting. It's been a profitable year, which is good, and I am learning new things every day. But what I try to teach people is, don't bet with emotion. Betting your favorite team is not necessarily the best way to go. Most people fall in love with a team and bet with their hearts instead of their heads. People always ask me who my favorite team is. My team is the New York Giants, but 90 percent of the time, I bet against them. My favorite team is the team that is going to cover the spread.

Sports betting is everywhere. Bet99.net is doing very well, and they are a great company to work for—very smart and very honest. There is going to be a television show in Quebec, and you bet that I'm looking forward to being involved with that.

CHAPTER 21

KILLER, BAM BAM, AND THE RAT

I GOT TO THE NHL because I was fearless.

I have thought about this since I retired. I would never have made the NHL—in fact, I never would have made Junior—if I hadn't adopted a persona and a style that opened the eyes of a lot of people.

I've always been an agitator. I was a mouthy kid who got beat up a lot in school. It's just my personality. I love teasing, whether it's my teammates, my friends, or my kids. And I hang out with the same kind of people. I get as good as I give. I was always running my mouth off, and then I had to suffer the consequences. So that was always part of me, but the fighting evolved.

I watched *Hockey Night in Canada* as a kid, staying up until 4:00 in the morning taping games. It was hockey, hockey, hockey, hockey for me. It's all I ever wanted to do. I wasn't really ready to play Junior, but that was my goal in life. I wanted to make it, but I realized after a couple of days at camp in Junior that I wasn't as physically strong as most of the other guys, who were a couple years older than me. I was a 17-year-old kid and still developing. My brother warned me that I'd have to stand out if I was going to make the team. He didn't tell me to fight, but it just sort of happened. I felt I wasn't good enough to stay on the team if I didn't have my own niche, so I adopted that personality of being the agitator, the guy who would take on any player, no matter how big or how good they were. It was an eye-opener for me. I thought, *Wow! The fans like this, my coach loves this, and my teammates think I'm a little squirrely, but they love it too!* And I realized I was getting a bit more space on the ice from opponents too. It became part of my game in Junior, and I took the same game to the NHL.

I was just in awe that I had gone from getting cut by teams to playing my first NHL game at 19 years old. And to do it in a tough, blue-collar town that really respected the way I played was awesome. I wanted to prove everyone wrong. There's nothing better in life than proving someone wrong. It's a motivating factor for me every day. I wouldn't have made Junior hockey and I wouldn't have made the NHL without that side of my game. You have to work hard and be in the right place at the right time, and those things aligned for me in Buffalo and allowed me to enjoy remarkable success. I call it luck, but everybody else says it's hard work that creates success. There is some of both that worked in my favor with the Sabres.

When I played Junior, I fought a lot and got the nickname Killer. It wasn't because I killed guys in fights but was more of a tag because I was willing to fight anyone. It didn't matter that I weighed 148 pounds my first year of Junior and was fighting guys 215, 220 pounds. I was fighting heavyweights such as Sandy McCarthy and Gino Odjick. It didn't matter. I wanted to stand out. Later, when I was playing in Buffalo, Danny Gare, who had retired after starring with the Sabres, was Buffalo's TV guy with Empire Sports. I fought somebody and Danny called me Bam Bam. No one in the room ever called me Bam Bam, but it stuck with some fans. Rick Jeanneret did play-by-play for the Sabres, and one day he said, "If Matthew Barnaby could fight with his mouth and his words, he'd be the heavyweight champion of the world. No one relishes being a rat more than Matthew Barnaby," and from that, Matt the Rat evolved. But again, no one on any of the teams I played for called me the Rat. It was another media nickname. To this day, the only guys who call me Killer are Doug Bodger, Dave Hannan, and Randy Moller. Everybody else I played with calls me Barney. Everyone.

I've got a tattoo on my arm. It reflects my NHL career. I've got the NHL logo and the years I played, then I've got KILLER, BAM BAM, and THE RAT beside it. I also have a landmark for each of the cities I played in.

In 1998 a *Hockey Night in Canada* feature called me the "most unpopular player in the NHL," and Scott Oake, the announcer, said that I don't play to rave reviews anywhere but in Buffalo. Don Cherry, when he was on *Hockey Night in Canada*, once said I was phony, and added, "The guy could be a good hockey player." And I have a long-running feud with Sean Avery, a rival irritant, who tells people I was "insane." Sure, I sometimes said things out there on the ice that I shouldn't have. I loved entertaining, and people paid a lot of money to watch us play. I wanted fans who came to watch us play feel like they got their money's worth.

I wear those nicknames and statements like badges of honor. I came to the rink every game and gave it my all. I stood up for my teammates, played hard on each shift, and entertained the fans.

*   *   *

In the 834 regular-season games I played in the NHL, I prepared for each one like it was going to be a schoolyard fight, knowing that I was probably going to have to square off against some really tough boys. In a schoolyard fight, you thought all day about what was going to happen after school, and once it happened, you might get a couple of scratches or bruises. But the stakes are a lot higher in the NHL.

I could never sleep the night before a game, knowing what was ahead. If we were playing Philadelphia, I knew I'd have to fight Donald Brashear. If it was Toronto, it'd be Tie Domi, and if it was the Rangers, I'd probably be fighting Ken Baumgartner. I knew that these were the guys I had to fight. These guys could do serious damage to your face or even end your career. I'd toss and turn, but the thoughts would haunt me, so I'd have a few beers or a few bottles of wine with the guys the night before. I wanted to put the possibilities of a fight as far from my mind as I could. Once I was in the moment in the game, I was having fun. I wasn't nervous anymore. I enjoyed it. The anticipation built through the game, so I liked to fight in my first or second shift of the game because I could get it over with and just play hockey.

Afternoon naps were the absolute worst, because I couldn't take my mind off what might happen during the game. I'd lie there picturing what five hours from then might look like. My mind would race and my palms would start to sweat. After an hour and a half of restlessness, I would get up, get dressed, pack up, find a Starbucks, and head off to the game. Once I got there, I was a different Matthew Barnaby.

One of my first games in the National Hockey League was against the Hartford Whalers. Stu Grimson had just been acquired by the Whalers. He was one of the toughest guys in the league. I did an interview before the game in Hartford and then went out for warm-up. Sometimes things happen in warm-up. Sometimes I would chirp at guys to get under their skin to set things up for the game. That night I was just skating, warming up, and I looked over and saw Stu Grimson glaring at me. He was not taking the customary line rushes that teams do during warm-ups. He wouldn't shoot a puck at his goalie, and he was standing at the red line, staring at me while he kicked the heels of his skates against the boards. *What the fuck is going on?* I thought. I didn't even know this guy! I had never played against him, and he was laser-focused on me, gritting his teeth. The opening faceoff took place, and I got my first shift when Grimson came at me. I didn't fight him and was trying to play my game. That whole game, he was chasing me. Finally, the last shift of the game, Stu was standing in the corner with the puck between his skates, daring me to come get it. I skated by and did a token swing.

I couldn't figure out why this guy wanted to kill me. Twenty-two years later, after having fought him a couple times during my career,

Stu called into a radio show I had on SiriusXM. "I'm hearing you talk, Barney, and I love ya. You were never afraid. But I've got to get something off my chest. Remember that time in Hartford at the start of your career? I had just been traded to Hartford, and Kelly Chase came up to me before the game and said, 'What the hell is with you and Barnaby?' I said, 'Nothing.' Chase said, 'I just heard him doing an interview, and he said, "Why the hell did the Whalers trade for Stu Grimson? He's not that tough, he can't skate, and he can barely play the game! They have enough tough guys over there, so why the hell did they trade for him?"'

Grimson said, "Really?" He and Chase walked out and saw me being interviewed, and he took Kelly Chase's comments at face value. But Kelly Chase is a prankster. He was lying to Grimson to get him fired up. And it worked! During that game, I went out for my first shift, and Grimson pulled one of his teammates off the ice so he could go out and confront me. That's when he started coming after me. He was going to murder me! Kelly waited 22 years to tell Stu the true story. When he called my radio show, he apologized, saying, "I'm sorry, man! I thought you said all those things about me, and you never said a word!"

There were guys I had no chance against. Stu Grimson was one. He was 6'5" and 235 pounds. I had no chance of hitting him. But it didn't mean that I didn't chirp at him. I'd go up to Stu before the game and tell him that he wasn't going to get to fight me because our coach didn't play me against fourth-liners. I taunted him, "If you can skate down and back without falling twice, I'll fight you. I've watched you for seven years and it hasn't happened yet!" Grimson would be spitting fire, waiting to get at me. I was fortunate. I got to play 13 minutes a night. I could play. I didn't have to fight. I did it as part of what I did in my game.

The heavyweights would be licking their chops waiting to fight me. I would do anything it took to get under the skin of the guys I was going to fight. I'd try to learn things about certain guys and use them to goad them into penalties. Donald Brashear, Stu Grimson, Andrei Nazarov, Krzysztof Oliwa—those boys hit me the hardest. They were so much bigger than me. I played at 188, and most of the heavyweights had 30 or more pounds on me. It didn't take much convincing to get them to go with me. What I would try to do was to draw them into penalties. I'd whack them in the back of the legs or say something to them. I'd be an idiot in any way that could get them to drop their gloves to go at me. We'd get a power play and score. All that mattered to me was winning. If I had to take a bruise, a slash, a punch to the back of the head, I did what I had to do, and Pat LaFontaine in Buffalo or Jaromir Jagr in Pittsburgh would go out and score on the power play. But I never wanted to be that guy who just draws guys into penalties. I would come back and give these guys the chance to beat the crap out of me. Hopefully I'd land some shots. I had to be willing to take 10 or 12 punches in order to get one in. I seldom was able to just go in there and stand in toe to toe. I had to think my way through a fight, tire the other guy out, and then get him at the end of the fight. They'd throw five or six punches and then they'd be tired. Once they started getting tired, then I'd throw a few jabs and look for the big one. You take some beatings, you take some concussions, but my primary goal was always to try to set guys up to take a penalty

There was a real fraternity among guys who fought in the NHL. We were competitors on the ice and there was no love lost, but off the ice was often a different story. Lyle Odelein was one of the few guys I hated on the ice. A few years ago, Tom McMillan, the PR guy for the Penguins, sent me a message to let me know that Lyle was in really bad shape. He had had a liver transplant and a kidney transplant. I didn't care about my feeling toward him and our history of fighting. I wished him well and am glad to say that he has recovered from his health crisis.

* * *

As a kid, I always wore No. 9. My number in Junior was 14. When I went to Buffalo, at training camp, they handed me 36. I was the kid with a mullet and half a front tooth just out of Junior. When I made the team, I kept the number. If I had had a choice, I would have taken 14, but Dave Hannan was already wearing it, and then it was retired for Rene Robert in 1995. My next choice would have been 9, but a guy named Viktor Gordiouk was wearing it. He only played 16 games the season I came up.

When I made the team in 1993–94, they asked me if I wanted to change numbers. Gordiouk was gone, so I said I'd love to wear No. 9, but then I stopped. "I can't," I said. I had watched so many fans buy my No. 36 jersey and thought that it would be shitty to change numbers on them, so I stuck with 36. That became my number. No one really wore that number back then, so that was the number I was known for and became my identity. I tried to wear it with every team I played for. I got traded to Colorado on March 8, 2004, and they told me that I couldn't wear 36. It was Steve Moore's number, and the incident with Todd Bertuzzi where Steve's career was ended was on March 9. It wouldn't have been right to take No. 36, so I told them to give me 37 or 38. It didn't matter. I got 38 with the Avalanche. I was only there for a couple months. And then when I went to Dallas, Jussi Jokinen had 36. I sat down with my wife and son to decide what number to wear. I wanted to choose a number as a family. We played a dice game and the number seven came up. My son was seven years old and blurted out, "How about 77, Dad? That would be so cool!" So 77 it was.

When my son started playing hockey, my wife asked what number Matthew should wear. She suggested 36, but I was definite: "No." I didn't want to put pressure on a kid who has to live up to his father's career. "Let him pick his own number," I said. "Let him create his own identity." In different seasons, he wore different numbers: 87 for Sidney Crosby, 88 for Patrick Kane, and then he settled on 9. I told him, "That number is going to look so good on you! You're a skilled player." He just looked at me and said, "Dad, I am wearing *your* number. Three plus six is nine!" Today with the Fort Wayne Komets he is wearing 37.

* * *

Between Junior, the AHL, and the NHL, I've had roughly 400 fights, of which about 200 were in the NHL. Every fight was calculated. I may have come off as a loose cannon and a lunatic, but I thought about the fights for hours, days, even months. But one thing I never thought about, on purpose, was concussions and their repercussions.

Scientists have studied concussions and found similarities among athletes who have suffered head trauma and varying degrees of brain damage. There is a long list of enforcers who died prematurely or had problems later in life. It's nerve-racking when you hear about these things happening to people. I don't think about the damage that head injuries have caused. That's just the way I live my life. Maybe when there is a story about a player such as Wade Belak or Derek Boogaard, I will think about CTE and the possible damage to brains from the punishment they've taken through the years. I'd be naive to think that there isn't a possibility that when it's my time, when they open me up and analyze my brain, I may very well have some CTE.

I was always cocky on the ice because that's the way I had to play, but when I left the rink, I was always a good guy to my friends and my family. After I retired in 2007, I lost that. I was short-tempered and irritable, and that certainly contributed to the ending of my marriage to Christine. I turned into a different man. I lost a sense of who I was for about two years. I didn't like the father I was becoming. I didn't like anything. The biggest part of me was that I would snap on anything. I was never one to snap off the ice. I got away from my family and the things I was proud of.

I am glad that the NHL has a concussion protocol now. We didn't really have one when I played, certainly not one like today. But there's nothing I can do about it now. Time will tell, but I can't live my life every day thinking I might die because of it. It's not the way I live my life. If I die a few years earlier, so be it. I've had a pretty damn good life.

Do I get more headaches than the average person? Probably, but I also think it might be because my shoulders are tight and tension goes up through my neck and causes headaches. I can say that the only thing I would see that I have because of fighting might be my short-term memory not being as sharp as it should be. But that could also be because through my entire life, I've gone a million miles an hour.

I hope Rhonda isn't wiping my ass before I'm 85, but after 85, she can wipe away.

*   *   *

If I could talk to the 14-year-old Matthew Barnaby today, I would tell him to stay true to himself and not fight as much. It's a crazy world out there. Follow your passions but beware of people who are trying to get things from you, who want to be friends with you because of who you are in name rather than the person you are. Be a good person. Avoid the mistakes that are out there. I didn't have a father to mentor me in these matters, but I can talk openly because I am a good person and I care about people. Despite the mistakes I've made, I'm happy with the way things have turned out.

Every Canadian kid dreams of playing in the NHL, and I was no different. I remembered doing a book report in sixth grade and said I was going to play for the Montreal Canadiens, buy a Lamborghini, and buy a house for my mother. One out of three happened, but it truly was a dream come true, especially after being cut twice in minor hockey. The dream of playing Junior seemed so far away, let alone ever playing in the National Hockey League.

I was laughed at by some kids in high school when I chose to work out rather than party, laughed at by teachers who told me that hockey would amount to nothing. Even family members—not my immediate family—talked about how delusional I was. I've always had a chip on my shoulder and wanted to prove people wrong. I'm not saying that's the only way, but it sure worked for me.

I wasn't special. I wasn't lucky. That took me a long time to understand. I knew what I wanted, was dedicated, and was willing to do whatever it took to achieve my goal. Success comes when hard work meets opportunity and the willingness to outwork others and do what they don't want to do. That's how I achieved my dream. Even though there were times when people didn't believe in me, and there were times I might have doubted myself, I found a way. Don't ever let anyone dictate your success or tell you that you're not good enough.

I was told by several people, including Ted Nolan, Pat LaFontaine, and Rob Ray, that I was a better player than I gave myself credit for. I finished my career with 113 goals and 300 points. I think I could have had 500 points had I not fought so much, but it is a big part of what got me to the NHL and why I stayed for as long as I did. I loved what I did, I loved the excitement I brought to the rink, I loved sticking up for my teammates. I wouldn't have been as effective a player if I hadn't done those things. And I wouldn't change a thing about the life I've lived.

EPILOGUE

Matthew was one of my favorite teammates I had during my 19-year NHL career. Not only were we brothers on the ice, but we remain great friends to this day. He has an uncanny ability to turn average situations into memorable and exciting moments. There is never a dull moment when Matthew is around. I love the guy and am blessed to have such a great friend.

Brad May
Buffalo Sabres teammate
1992–93 to 1997–98

As polarizing and as unpredictable as Matthew Barnaby was to hockey fans, the exact opposite stood true of him as a friend and a teammate. Very few teammates were as loyal and as protective as Matt. Competing alongside him allowed players to always feel comfortable on the ice and play to their top ability in a generation of hockey that was near physical madness every night.

Jay McKee
Buffalo Sabres teammate
1995–96 to 1998–99

Everybody who plays in the NHL has a story of where they are from, how they got there, and what kept them in the league. Matthew Barnaby was one of those players with a story that should inspire any boy or girl to never give up on their dreams. Through sheer grit and determination, Matthew defied all odds to become an NHL player. Hidden behind the combative style he displayed was a player with great hockey sense and an underrated skill set. Matthew was not perfect and made mistakes like us all, but what I found in Matthew was a person and teammate who loved the game, competed every night, and displayed courage that inspired his own teammates to play harder for each other.

Mark Messier
New York Rangers teammate
2001–02 to 2003–04

Matthew Barnaby—where do I start? Being in the National Hockey League for 26 years, I was very lucky to have some of the best and nicest players come through my dressing room door. Matthew was at the top of the list. What you saw on the ice wasn't how he was in the dressing room. He is one first-class person—very considerate of others, and he always treated his trainers with the utmost of respect. If anything needed to be said in the room, he had no problem being that leader that teams need. It was a joy to have him in Pittsburgh. He always had time for everyone, loved to sit and have a coffee on game days, and loved to talk about Sunday football games. His line to me was always, "Who do you like today, Steve?" I can't say enough about him. I was lucky to spend the time I did with him. I wish it had been longer. True professional and one great guy.

Steve Latin
Trainer
Pittsburgh Penguins

Matt came to the Buffalo Sabres as a skinny 19-year-old kid. He was one of my favorites during my time as the team's head trainer. He surprised everyone by how tough he was. He had one big problem: he feared no one! That made it tough on guys like Brad May and Rob Ray, because during their careers, both of them had players they didn't want to fight, but Matt didn't. Pound for pound, he was the toughest player in the NHL. He usually never fought guys his size; he fought the other team's heavyweight. Matt was a great team player and would do anything to win. It was a sad day for me when he was traded.

Jim Pizzutelli
Trainer
Buffalo Sabres

Acknowledgments

Matthew Barnaby

Writing this book has been absolutely awesome. Not only did it bring back amazing memories, but it also gave me a chance to reflect on my life: the past, the present, and what I want in the future. None of this would have been possible without an amazing family, because without their unwavering support from a very young age, I would never have been able to accomplish my goal of playing in the National Hockey League.

Mom:

My mother sacrificed and did everything for me. She was selfless in providing for me, caring for me, and somehow finding the money to allow me to do what I loved. I know how hard it must have been, but never did she complain. Mom, I thank you for all you have ever done, and it is appreciated beyond the words I can write. I love you and thank you for being my biggest supporter both in good times and bad.

Nanny:

I got my fierce competitiveness from my grandmother. You hated to lose and were an angel. I spent so much time with you while growing up and cherished every moment. Thank you for being the best, Nanny. I miss you every day.

Brent:

My brother. The one person who loves hockey more than me. Thank you for spending day after day taking me to hockey and putting me before anything, for believing in me when no one else believed in me. Thank you for pushing me and being very honest when honesty was needed. Without you, there is zero chance that I would have made Junior hockey, let alone the NHL.

Christine:

You raised two unbelievably loving children. You let me concentrate on my work and took care of everything else so I never had to worry about anything except playing hockey. I know I wasn't always easy, but I really appreciated the support you gave me and, most of all, our family we created.

Rhonda:

My life is as good as it's ever been, and that's in large part because I have you. The love, the laughs, the experiences, and how you push and believe in me makes me strive to be better every day. We have known each other since we were 17. You were my best friend then and you're still my best friend today. They say you tease the ones you love most. Well, if that's true, we are really in love! Thank you for allowing me on the "crazy train." Here's to many more years. You are my "ride or die." Love from Rocket 36.

Matthew and Taylor:

My Bear and my Princess. You will find this out one day, but there is no love like the love you have for your children. You two are my everything. My highest of highs come when you are happy. Nothing can compare. I am so incredibly proud of you both. I am proud of your accomplishments but more so of the people you have become: loving, caring, and compassionate. I have made mistakes—many of them—but through all of them, I want you to know that it was hurting you or embarrassing you that hurt me the most. I love you both unconditionally and thank you for the joy, the love, and the amazing feeling I get every day from being your dad. I love you both to infinity and beyond.

Taylor, some of my greatest memories were watching you at dance classes from the time you were five. You were so little and scared, standing there crying at your dance recital. I remember trying my best to do your hair for you before school, only to have the teacher redo it for you. And I laugh with so much love thinking about taking you to buy cleats and hair bands that would match your soccer jersey.

Matthew, we've had so much fun together through the years. I think about you being excited to play in "pampionships" because you couldn't say "championships." If we played games together, I never let you win, and you were so competitive that you'd snap. I watched you discreetly throw away second-place trophies because if you didn't win, you didn't want them. And some of my fondest memories are taking you to early morning skates on outdoor rinks and sitting in my car with the lights on so you could train before school.

Alain Chainey:

You believed in a skinny English kid who was out of his element. You were patient and gave me an opportunity. In sports, but even more in life, you need someone to believe in you. Thank you for believing in me.

Ted Nolan:

You let me be *me*—outspoken and sometimes a little crazy, and understood that for me to be my best, I had to be those things. Thank you for your trust and loyalty and for being there for me for more than just hockey.

Kevin Shea:

Thank you for taking my words and capturing my true personality. I wanted to be true to myself and who I am. Thank you for all your time. Going through the process with you was very rewarding. I hope you enjoyed it as much as I did and are equally as proud.

The Fans:

Thank you from the bottom of my heart, especially Buffalo fans, for embracing me and supporting me. I couldn't have asked for a more perfect fan base to be drafted to. It was like it was meant to be. Pittsburgh and the Barnaby Brigade: it was hard being traded, but to go to a place that was so passionate about their team made the transition easy. And New York: there is only one Madison Square Garden, and the chants of "Potvin sucks," plus the goal song going off, still give me chills. I wish we had had more success, but Rangers fans are nuts, and I loved it!

Lastly, to all the other fans who hated me, especially the Flyers fans: you motivated me but also made it fun. Sports are all about competition and loving your team. Flyers fans are as passionate and crazy as any fans. From the death threats to the "Fuck you, Barnaby" chants—I loved every minute of it, understood it, and if I didn't hear them, I wasn't doing my job. I should have been a Flyer at some point. That would have been epic! So one last "Fuck you" to you guys!

KEVIN SHEA

I certainly knew Matthew from watching games on television, but I only met Matthew in person when I invited him to be one of our celebrities at a fundraising event in Toronto called Road Hockey to Conquer Cancer. Matthew was an amazing ambassador, so when he contacted me about working with him on his autobiography, I was quick to accept, and I thank Matthew for giving me this opportunity. Huge thanks to the great staff at Triumph Books for their support. I appreciated the additional support from Ted Nolan, Mark Messier, Eric Lindros, the Hockey Hall of Fame and, on a personal level, my wife, Nancy Niklas, and my brother, Dale Shea, who are always supportive of my writing endeavors.